Frank Reimers

Security Culture in Times of War:
How did the Balkan War affect the Security Cultures
in Germany and the United States?

Security Culture in Times of War: How did the Balkan War affect the Security Cultures in Germany and the United States?

Frank Reimers

2020

Carola Hartmann Miles-Verlag Berlin

Bibliografische Information der Deutschen Nationalbibliothek
Die Deutsche Nationalbibliothek verzeichnet diese Publikation in der Deutschen Nationalbibliografie; detaillierte bibliografische Daten sind im Internet über www.dnb.de abrufbar.

© 2020 Carola Hartmann Miles-Verlag, Berlin
www.miles-verlag.jimdo.com
E-Mail: miles-verlag@t-online.de

Herstellung: Books on Demand, Norderstedt

Printed in Germany

ISBN 978-3-96776-006-4

To my father

TABLE OF CONTENTS

INTRODUCTION

World politics have undergone an unanticipated and unprecedented diplomatic and strategic revolution since 1989, the year that ushered in a new era of rapid change. New political actors appeared within and on the horizon of Europe. Security issues that had dominated policy for over forty years suddenly disappeared. Theories of International Relations were challenged to explain and interpret breathtaking and puzzling new events. Realist and neo-liberalist assumptions of rational, unitary actors with interests predetermined by the balance of power were challenged by constructivist and culturalist approaches focused on the social construction of actors' identities and interests. Some of the puzzles for realists and neo-liberals could be explained by those theories.

Exploring the political culture of international actors helps to clarify diverging policies and increases the chance of success in politics, while decreasing the risks of misperception, miscommunication and flawed policies. Culture helps orient people to the political environment. It shapes and constrains the behavior and interests of political actors. The post-Cold War era thus requires rethinking and reorienting international relations. This is particularly relevant to the increasingly shared security culture among actors in the transitional process. The basic insight is this: culture matters in world politics.

This thesis illustrates how Euro-Atlantic security cultures have adjusted to the post-Cold War environment. The thesis explores the security culture of Germany and the United States during the war in Bosnia-Herzegovina, beginning in 1992 and ending with the Dayton Peace Accords of 1995. Examining the Bosnian war and its effect on the German and the American security culture provides a better understanding of the causal impact of crises and political shocks on international actors, their subsequent internal change, and the implications of changing security culture on the preferences and behavior of international actors.

The findings of this thesis might provide scholars and policymakers with novel insights on the evolution of security cultures and the ramifications of this process for international relations.

In recent years, security cultures, often called strategic cultures, have become the focus of serious research efforts by scholars of war and peace. There is wide-ranging theoretical and empirical disagreement among such scholars on pivotal issues. A major disagreement concerns the dynamic understanding of cultures. Earlier research, assuming coherent and stable cultural entities, held that security culture is resistant to change. More recent research highlights the dynamic nature of security cultures, linking culture and behavior, as one scholar writes, "by considering culture as practice."[1] The literature argues that security cultures evolve, sometimes slowly and incrementally, other times rapidly in the wake of a defining event. This thesis follows those scholars who emphasize the dynamics of security cultures, analyzing their emergence and transformation, their path-dependence and boundaries.

It is of both academic interest and political importance to reveal the causal mechanisms linking security culture and political behavior. The case studies of Germany and the United States demonstrate that security cultures influence the assessment of political situations, restrain policy objectives, and condition the range of issues to which political attention is devoted. Both case studies reveal that a changing security culture affects the evaluation of available policy options and the choices that are made. Security culture thus predisposes the behavior of key actors and institutions.

The German case study suggests that the option to use military force during the first years of the Bosnian war was simply rejected by leading elites as inappropriate, even taboo. The prevailing security culture in Germany derived from the experience of World War II and Federal Republic of Germany's (FRG) political culture in the Cold War. The horrendous war atrocities in Bosnia after 1992 triggered a substantial change in German views on the use of force among both political elites and society as a whole. For the United States, on the other hand, the option of forceful and effective intervention in European affairs was at the outset simply not imagined by

---

[1] Darryl Howlett, "Strategic Culture: Reviewing Recent Literature," *Strategic Insights* 4, no.10 (2005), 7, http://www.ccc.nps.navy.mil/si/2005/Oct/howlettOct05.asp, accessed 30 August 2006.

the George H. W. Bush administration, which adhered to the political status quo of an intact Yugoslavia and had strategic concerns about the dissolving Soviet Union and the Persian Gulf. The policy changed with the presidency of Bill Clinton. The case study examines whether the Bosnian war affected the U.S. security culture itself, or only shifted policies towards more effective intervention.

Broad scholarly research on the German security culture emerged after unification, but little research is available on the security culture of the United States in regard to the wars in former Yugoslavia.

Given that security cultures condition political action and influence and frame policy options, this thesis aims specifically to enhance our understanding of German and U.S. foreign policies. The thesis analyzes the political motivations and choices of the two states during the war, arguing that the transformation of their respective security cultures led to diverging political behavior. The domestic feedback of the Bosnian war transformed German security culture and to a lesser extend the American, particularly with regard to the use of force. This resulted in more forceful and effective interventions in Bosnia and has framed the future of both countries' interventions in conflicts. Understanding how security cultures change and evolve through exogenous and endogenous factors increases the chances of policy success, so this thesis might improve policy in today's challenging international environment.

To address how the war in Bosnia changed German and American security cultures, the thesis treats the Bosnian war as an enduring political shock experience with far-ranging repercussions on German and U.S. society and political elites, considering how the war reoriented both security cultures and changed policy choices. The thesis focuses on two components of security cultures, the shared perception of the use of force and multilateralism. It argues that within a few years, German perception of military force changed considerably to favor effective and legitimate deployment of German forces beyond national territory and treaty obligations. The thesis demonstrates that the security culture of the United States also shifted as a result of the international environment, from abstention in the early 1990s to a more effective and intensive intervention in European affairs. All in all, the thesis aims to shed light on how security cultures change due to external shocks.

This thesis tests how national security cultures impact the political preferences and choices of international actors. The dependent variables (DV) are changes in U.S. and German security cultures; the independent variable (IV) is the Bosnian war. Intervening variables (Int V) are factors that mediate between the Bosnian war and domestic security culture, i.e. which cause the war to have an impact on societal and elite predispositions. These factors center on crises and formative events.[2] The thesis assumes that only those international events perceived as very profound and challenging can change national security cultures.[3] To have an impact, the Bosnian war had to be collectively perceived as a crisis by the publics and elites in the U.S. and Germany. Major intervening variables which exposed the public and the leadership to the war include personal contacts with the war zone through visits or the testimony of refugees, as well as exposure to the war through the mass media and the so-called "CNN effect."[4] The change of security cultures is assumed to have caused a transformation of interests, norms and behavior.

Chapter II of the thesis examines the concept of security cultures, focusing on the process of change. After presenting the general concept and the problem of heterogeneity, it discusses how, and how

---

[2] In this thesis, crises and formative events are defined differently. The entire Bosnian war is conceptualized as a crisis from the U.S. and German perspective. The war unfolded as a sequence of formative events understood as single incidents with singular, but interrelated impacts (e.g. Srebrenica).

[3] Cognitive consistency theory assumes that individuals make sense of the world by relying on key beliefs and strive to maintain consistency between their beliefs. Individuals maintain coherent belief systems and avoid exposure to information that is inconsistent or incompatible with their beliefs. Thus, belief systems are resistant to most external events. However, should change occur, the abrupt and all-encompassing nature of belief systems changes also. See Jerel A. Rosati, "A Cognitive Approach to the Study of Foreign Policy," in *Foreign Policy Analysis, Continuity and Change in Its Second Generation*, edited by Laura Neack, Jeanne A. K. Hey, and Patrick J. Haney (Englewood Cliffs: Prentice Hall, 1995), 52- 63.

[4] Viktor Meier, "Die politische Bedeutung der Medien in der Konfliktbewaeltigung," in *Deutsche Konfliktbewaeltigung auf dem Balkan. Erfahrungen und Lehren aus dem Einsatz*, edited by Rafael Biermann (Baden-Baden: Nomos, 2002), 139-150.

much, security cultures change. Chapter III tracks the internal developments and events in Bosnia in between 1992 and 1995 to establish the factual background.

Subsequent chapters concentrate on the impact of these events on the security cultures of Germany (Chapter IV) and the United States (Chapter V), looking at both political elites and society in general. Chapter VI compares the case studies to determine if values are congruent or incongruent with the concept of security culture and the assumptions of this thesis. Chapter VII concludes this thesis with a discussion of the implications of the findings for the concept of security culture. The basic testing method consists of paired observations. For the controlled comparison, data from both cases is passively observed. The thesis employs process tracing to examine the nature and quantity of changes. The outcome of the examination is closely related to national dispositions.

The two cases diverge considerably. German and American history and politics differ dramatically. At the beginning of the conflict, the two nations had almost contradictory security cultures and opinions on the use of force and crisis management. Germany was diplomatically proactive in 1991, during the first phase of the conflict, while after an initial probe the U.S. refrained from even diplomatic interference. However, both nations abstained from military intervention at the beginning and later became fully involved in peace enforcement, with pivotal roles in the peace settlement (Dayton) and post-conflict peace building phases (Dayton implementation). This reveals a convergence, not only of policies but also of cultures.

The case studies demonstrate that exogenous factors caused by the Bosnian war triggered a change of elite and popular norms and beliefs. This led to more effective crisis management, even though at the outset of the crisis the German and American predispositions and perceptions of exogenous factors differed tremendously.

Using changes in security culture as a dependent variable is a challenge for research. Security cultures are hard to measure and observe.[5] Therefore, this thesis researches so-called culture-bearing units, focusing mainly on political elites and the general population. Security cultures are expressed, recorded and sometimes codified in discourse, opinion polls and political behavior. Thus, the thesis relies on the externalities of culture, i.e., on observable discourse and opinions rather than on culture itself. Primary sources for the elite level are speeches, memoirs, interviews and legislative hearings, while sources for the general society include opinion polls and domestic laws, institutions and regulations that reflect cultural changes.

---

[5] Theo Farrel, "Constructivist Security Studies: Portrait of a Research Program," *International Studies Review* 4, no.1 (2002), 60.

II.   THE CONCEPT OF SECURITY CULTURE

There is considerable scholarly literature on security cultures.[6] It emerged in the 1970s. The first generation of scholarly work, launched by the U.S. political scientist Jack Snyder, applied the political culture argument to security studies in the final phases of the Cold War.[7] Snyder argued that rhetoric by political elites reflects a distinctive security culture which in turn reflects the beliefs of a whole society.[8] The second generation of security culture researchers generally used Snyder's contributions to examine superpower relations and nuclear strategy. Other scholars linked national styles, civic culture and ways of life to Snyder's findings.[9] In the wake of the profound political transformation of the 1990s, cultural interpretations were rediscovered by a third generation of political scholars. Constructivists like Alexander Wendt pointed to the impact of social structures, including norms, identity, and ideas, on the behavior of states or international relations.[10] The diversity of academic discourse is now immense, with disagreements about theoretical concepts, definitions and analytical approaches to the topic. On the other hand, the study of culture incorporates many insights from other disciplines, including sociology, anthropology and social psychology.

---

[6] Elizabeth L. Stone, Christopher P. Twomey, and Peter R. Lavoy, "Comparative Strategic Culture," *Strategic Insights* 4, no.10 (2005), http://www.ccc.nps.navy.mil/events/recent/ComparativeStrategicCultureSep05rpt.asp, accessed 30 Aug. 2006.

[7] Jeffrey S. Lantis, "Strategic Culture From Clausewitz to Constructivism," *Strategic Insights* 4, no. 10 (2005), 2, http://www.ccc.nps.navy.mil/si/2005/Oct/lantisOct05.asp, accessed 30 Aug. 2006.

[8] Jack Snyder, *The Soviet Strategic Culture: Implications for Nuclear Options*, report number R-2154-AF (Santa Monica, Calif.: Rand Cooperation, 1977), 8.

[9] Lantis, "Strategic Culture From Clausewitz to Constructivism," 3.

[10] Lantis, "Strategic Culture From Clausewitz to Constructivism," 3.

A.   DIFFERENTIATION AND DEFINITION

To distance themselves from rationalist theories of international relations, constructivist and culturalist theorists merged the concepts of security and culture. Theo Farrel argues that actors are located in a social structure "that both constitutes those actors and is constituted by their interaction."[11] The basic logic behind the constructivist theory is that culture plays an important role in international politics. Alastair Iain Johnston opines that decision-makers, both cross-nationally and over time, think and act differently when faced with similar circumstances because strategic realities are perceived differently.[12] The gap between situation and response is caused by the "subjective processing of experiences," which explains why perception matters in politics and consequently in international relations.[13]

The studies of political culture have an affinity with studies of ideas and beliefs, but are more comprehensive. Definitions of the term "political culture" may be broad or narrow. In the 1960s, Almond and Verba defined political culture as a "subset of beliefs and values of a society that relate to the political system."[14] Other scholars equate culture with a collective "mind set,"[15] conceptualized as general dispositions of actors and orientations towards action.[16] John S. Duffield defines political culture as "the subjective and often unquestioned orientations toward and assumptions about the political world that characterize the members of a particular society or social unit and that guide and inform their behavior."[17] He argues that political culture consists of three components: the cognitive, which includes causal beliefs; the evaluative, which includes values and norms; and

---

[11] Farrel, 49-72.

[12] Alistair Iain Johnston, "Thinking about Strategic Culture," *International Security* 19, no. 4 (Spring 1995), 35-55.

[13] Harry Eckstein, "A Culturalist Theory of Political Change," *American Political Science Review* 82, no. 3 (Sept. 1998), 790.

[14] Quoted in Lantis, "Strategic Culture From Clausewitz to Constructivism," 2.

[15] Johnston, 45.

[16] Eckstein, 790.

[17] John S. Duffield, *World Power Forsaken: Political Culture, International Institutions and German Security Policy After Unification.* (Stanford: Stanford University Press, 1998), 23.

18

the affective, which includes emotional attachments, patterns of identity and loyalty, and feelings of affinity.[18] In other words, political cultures predispose societies and their political representatives to certain behaviors in international politics. This thesis uses the concept of security culture defined by Duffield. Security culture consists of cognitive, affective and evaluative predispositions which shape foreign and security perceptions and policies of a collective entity.[19]

B. HETEROGENEITY AND SOURCES OF SECURITY CULTURES

Security cultures are shaped through material and ideational factors.[20] Howlett outlines four essential sources. First, geography and natural resources are key elements in shaping and transforming security cultures. Geographical proximity to great powers, along with contested and unresolved national border problems, accounts for differing state security perceptions.[21] A second source of security culture is history and experience. Historical lessons learned by political elites and actors and recent experiences do have a striking effect on the security culture and cause path dependence. A third source refers to the internal political structure of a state, e.g. the type of regime. Finally, the institutional framework of a state significantly influences security cultures. Institutions can develop unique organizational cultures which spill over and shape national security cultures.

Scholars differ on how much homogeneity is needed to speak of one culture. During the Cold War, scholars around the world spoke of two cultures, the American and the Soviet cultures.[22] That surely was a simplification. Further examination shows that individuals have different orientations[23] and learn different things from expe-

---

18 Duffield, 23.

19 Duffield, 24.

20 Howlett, 4.

21 Howlett, 4.

22 Johnston, 37.

23 Eckstein, 792.

rience.[24] Thus, societies contain "multiple strategic cultures,"[25] since societies encompass various subcultures. Heterogeneity and homogeneity exist side by side, and the facts often show a dominant, hegemonic culture as well as competing ones.[26] Thus it is necessary to examine which group actually shapes the security culture of a country.

Another debate in the literature deals with the universality and boundaries of security cultures. The classical approach to research is individual country studies, with comparative studies appearing more rarely. Researchers differ on how far security cultures can also be perceived as transnational phenomena. If the latter is the case, then cultures encompass not only states but also regions and even non-state actors, such as Al Quaeda.[27]

The cultural effect of interdependence, globalization and integration is not yet much a part of the academic discourse. The question remains, do states share a common security culture because of parallel identity formation processes? For example, do liberal democracies perceive themselves as an "in-group?"[28] This issue is of great relevance for security communities and democratic peace. Transnationalism raises the question of where to draw the boundaries of cultures.[29] Nonetheless, universality and the boundaries of security cultures deserve more research.

C.   CONTINUITY AND CHANGE

The discourse about the change of cultures is controversial. Some scholars argue that cultures are persistent, static and even resistant to transformation.[30] Others argue that political cultures are dynamic. While change is normally slow and incremental, it evolves in phases

---

[24] Jack S. Levy, "Learning and Foreign Policy: Sweeping a Conceptual Minefield," *International Organization* 48, no. 2 (Spring 1994), 300.

[25] Johnston, 38.

[26] Howlett, 10.

[27] Lantis, "Strategic Culture From Clausewitz to Constructivism," 9-10.

[28] Johnston, 61.

[29] Howlett, 3.

[30] Stone, Twomey and Lavoy, 8-9.

of rest, acceleration and deceleration.[31] The slow incremental change of security cultures is caused by learning through a continuous process of internalization and socialization[32] which is transmitted through time. This internalization of security cultures is decisive; it acts as a filter insofar as it conditions later learning. In other words, internalization creates and transforms dispositions that accumulate over time in the form of security cultures. Cognitive, affective, and evaluative components of learning interact in this process.

Harry Eckstein emphasizes that besides "normal" incremental change, a second mode of transformation might occur, triggered by great forces which "induce great changes in direction and velocity."[33] A similar view is presented by Duffield, confirming that traumatic experiences and crises discredit core beliefs and values and modify a security culture.[34] Gary Goertz and Paul Diehl broaden the discussion about crises and political shocks by distinguishing between system shocks and state shocks in their analysis of enduring rivalries.[35] Critical junctures represent defining events. They induce policy choices, with a path-dependent effect.[36] Initial choices determine future policy trajectories and outcomes, since choices foreclose some options while opening others. In other words, formative events are rare and sudden, but have a lasting impact.

A useful tool for exploring the change of political cultures is the concept of "learning through failure." Jack S. Levy argues that people learn more from failure than from success. Unanticipated and unintended negative experience stimulates policy debates about lessons from history and motivates change. He also argues that people

---

[31] Eckstein, 793.

[32] Eckstein, 802.

[33] Eckstein, 793.

[34] Duffield, 6-23.

[35] Gary Goertz and Paul F. Diehl, "The Initiation and Termination of Enduring Rivalries: The Impact of Political Shocks," *American Journal of Political Science* 39, no. 1 (1995) 30-52.

[36] Stephen Krasner, "Approaches to the State: Alternative Conceptions and Alternative Dynamics," *Comparative Politics* 16, no. 2 (1984), 240-244.

learn more from their own experience than from others'.[37] This generalization has merit for understanding war, peace, security, and defense in Germany and the U.S. in the twentieth century, when strategic trauma of varying sorts loomed large.

D.   GERMANY AND THE UNITED STATES

Linking culture and politics has become more popular.[38] But how are culture and politics causally related? Duffield argues that five causal mechanisms link national security culture and politics: security cultures condition the range of issues to which political attention is devoted, influence the diagnosis of political situations, help to determine policy objectives, shape the formulation and identification of policy options, and influence the evaluation of available policy options and thus the choices made. The overall effect is to predispose societies in general and political elites in particular towards specific actions and policies over others. Some options will simply not be imagined. Of those that are contemplated, some are more likely to be rejected as inappropriate or ineffective than others.[39]

Other scholars are less sophisticated in describing the linkage of security culture and politics, arguing simply that security cultures frame choices, that culture limits behavioral choices and creates preferences or that security cultures are preconditions of political actions.

Because few issues of foreign policy in recent history have evoked so much division, emotion, and disillusionment as the wars in former Yugoslavia, an enormous literature has emerged since the middle 1990s. Research focuses on the historical context, causes of the conflict, its internal evolution and the conflict resolution efforts of the international community. The failure of national actors and international organizations to prevent violent conflict and enforce peace is a prevalent theme. In her groundbreaking book *Balkan Tragedy*, Susan Woodward researched the impact of the Bosnian war on the international environment and outside actors. Woodward argues that

---

[37] Levy, 279-312.

[38] Lantis, "Strategic Culture From Clausewitz to Constructivism," 2.

[39] Duffield, 26-27.

"failure arose from a lack of understanding of the causes of the conflict, and the application of Cold War thinking and instruments that were not appropriate to the case."[40] This analysis naturally raises questions about how particular national security cultures contributed to the situation, and at what cost.

Others, including James Gow, analyzed "the involvement of the international community in trying to end the war and the overall failure of those efforts."[41] Gow demonstrates in his book that the main failures of the international community which led to the savage war were the lack of political will to use force, insufficient international cohesion and misperceptions. Christopher Bennet examined the war from another perspective, arguing that the constitutional arrangements in Yugoslavia under Tito were well-designed in regard to the relations between the Yugoslav people. Those arrangements were the best, and possibly the only formula for national coexistence in multiethnic Yugoslavia after World War II. Bennet argues that "there are rational explanations for everything which has taken place" in the breakup of Yugoslavia.[42]

Other literature focuses more generally on the Balkan region. Dunja Melcic's edited volume analyzes in detail many aspects of the historical and cultural context of this complex conflict.[43] Another line of research examines international crisis management. Thomas R. Mockaitis focuses on the efforts and failures of the United Nations in former Yugoslavia prior to 1995.[44]

A major contribution to the literature on German foreign policy is *Strategic Dilemmas and the Evolution of German Foreign Policy Since*

---

[40] Susan Woodward, *Balkan Tragedy: Chaos and Dissolution after the Cold War* (Washington D.C.: Brookings Institution, 1995), vii.

[41] James Gow, *Triumph of the Lack of Will: International Diplomacy and the Yugoslav War* (New York: Columbia University Press, 1997), v.

[42] Christopher Bennet, *Yugoslavia's Bloody Collapse Causes Course and Consequences* (New York: New York University Press, 1995), viii.

[43] Dunja Melcic, *Der Jugoslawienkrieg Handbuch zur Vorgeschichte und Konsequenzen* (Wiesbaden: Westdeutscher Verlag, 1999), 12.

[44] Thomas R. Mockaitis, *Peace Operations and Intrastate Conflict: The Sword or the Olive Branch* (Westport: Praeger Publishers, 1999), x.

Unification by Jeffrey S. Lantis.[45] The main argument of his chapter on the Bosnian war is that the crisis in former Yugoslavia served as a catalyst to change German foreign and security policy. The strategic dilemmas during the war accelerated the discourse about German responsibility in world affairs, which culminated in the use of military force. Lantis, though, does not take a constructivist view. Other important literature discusses international public opinion during the Bosnia crisis.[46] Karin Johnston's "German Public Opinion and the Crisis in Bosnia" highlights public opinion throughout the crisis and how it influenced German politics. Like Lantis, she does not connect her findings to theory about culture. The theoretical aspects are covered in the book *World Power Forsaken* by Duffield.[47]

There is huge body of literature about the security culture of the United States. The main literature focuses on the U.S. security culture in the nuclear age of the Cold War. Snyder studied the Soviet military strategy in 1977 in the context of the U.S. deterrence doctrine through the lens of security culture.[48] The strategic studies field is strongly influenced by Snyder's work. Colin S. Gray says "there are distinctive U.S. and Soviet national styles in nuclear strategy, [and] those styles are comprehensible on the basis of historical and anthropological understanding."[49] Ken Booth demonstrates the importance of security cultures in multiple policy areas and its implications by providing "[the] first extensive examination of the relationship between ethnocentrism and strategy."[50] But even more recent literature does not discuss the specific repercussions of the Bosnian war on

---

[45] Jeffrey S. Lantis, *Strategic Dilemmas and the Evolution of German Foreign Policy Since Unification* (Westport: Praeger Publishers, 2002).

[46] See Karin Johnston, "German Public Opinion and the Crisis in Bosnia," *International Public Opinion and the Bosnia Crisis,* edited by Richard Sobel and Eric Shiraev (New York: Lexington Books, 2003), 249-281.

[47] Duffield.

[48] Snyder.

[49] Colin S. Gray, *Nuclear Strategy and National Style* (Lanham, MD: Hamilton Press, 1986), ix.

[50] Ken Booth, *Strategy and Ethnocentrism* (New York: Holmes and Meyer Publishers, 1979), 10.

American security culture. The constructivist approach to cultures and especially the concept of learning through failure are not covered at all.

No comparative research has yet been done on the security cultures of Germany and the United States. Duffield's work on the German security culture links German foreign policy restraints with the constructivist findings of culture.[51] Lantis examines the evolution of the German security culture during the Kosovo War.[52] Neither examines the specific repercussions of the Bosnian war on the German security culture. The security culture of the United States is normally viewed from a realist perspective. An exception is Colin Dueck's book *Reluctant Crusaders,* which examines the changing U.S. security culture from a realist perspective and compares it with a domestic cultural explanation, concluding that U.S. foreign policy choices can best be explained by realist concepts.[53]

Another contribution is to the literature is Michael Lind's argument, in *The American Way of Strategy*, that "the purpose of the American way of strategy has always been to defend the American way of life."[54]

In sum, there is a large literature on the security cultures of Germany and the U.S. The literature on the U.S. focuses primarily on the Cold War and the nuclear age. The Cold War realist perspectives still dominate scholarly work since the collapse of the Soviet Union. The more recent literature on German security culture views the concept of security cultures from a constructivist perspective.

---

[51] Duffield.

[52] Jeffrey S. Lantis, "The Moral Imperative of Force: The Evolution of German Strategic Culture in Kosovo," *Comparative Strategy*, no. 21 (2002).

[53] Colin Dueck, *Reluctant Crusaders Power, Culture, and Change in American Grand Strategy* (Princeton: Princeton University Press, 2006), 5.

[54] Michael Lind, *The American Way of Strategy* (New York: Oxford University Press, 2006), 5.

III. THE BOSNIAN WAR

The Balkan wars followed the weakening of the Communist system after the Cold War.[55] What began as an acute crisis of post communism in southern Europe became a threat to the peace of Europe. The conflict proved a classical example of state transformation from socialism and one party rule to free market democracy. The causal cluster for the breakup, made possible only by the end of the Cold War, could be described as "economic discontent expressed through ethnic and national differences due to the unique nature of the federated state."[56] The communist party of Yugoslavia lost its ideological cohesion and gave way to nationalist and separatist ideologies that first plagued the Kingdom of the Serbs, Croat and Slovenes in the 1920s and later, in World War II, became a source of genocidal fury. Strong nationalist and separatist movements were present in Croatia, Serbia, and Bosnia-Herzegovina and to a lesser extent in Slovenia and Macedonia.

The state of Yugoslavia was formally dissolved on January 15, 1992 when the European Community officially recognized the republics of Croatia and Slovenia as sovereign states. Following their example, Bosnia held an independence referendum in later that year and

---

[55] On the Bosnian war this author relied primarily on following works: Mark Almond, *Europe's Backyard War: The War in the Balkans* (London: Mandarin Paperbacks, 1994); Christopher Bennett, *Yugoslavia's Bloody Collapse Causes, Course and Consequences* (New York: New York University Press, 1995); Rafael Biermann, *Lehrjahre im Kosovo: Das Scheitern der internationalen Krisenprävention vor Kriegsausbruch* (Paderborn: Ferdinand Schöningh, 2006); Ivo H. Daalder, *Getting to Dayton: The Making of America's Bosnia Policy* (Washington, D.C.: Brookings Institution Press, 2000); James Gow, *Triumph of the Lack of Will: International Diplomacy and the Yugoslav War* (New York: Columbia University Press, 1997); Richard C. Holbrooke, *To End a War* (New York: Random House, 1998); Dunja Melcic, ed., *Der Jugoslawien-Krieg: Handbuch zu Vorgeschichte, Verlauf und Konsequenzen* (Opladen/Wiesbaden: Westdeutscher Verlag GmbH, 1999); Thomas R. Mockaitis, *Peace Operations and Intrastate Conflict, The Sword or the Olive Branch* (Westport: Praeger Publishers, 1999); Laura Silber and Alan Little, *Yugoslavia: Death of a Nation* (New York: TV Books, 1996); Susan L. Woodward, *Balkan Tragedy: Chaos and Dissolution after the Cold War* (Washington, D.C.: Brookings Institution, 1995).

[56] Mockaitis, 81.

declared its independence in March 1992. Fighting broke out when the Yugoslav National Army (JNA), having decades earlier evolved into an instrument of Serb supremacy, moved into Slovenia in June 1991 to avert "secession." Violent clashes followed in the Serb-inhabited areas of Croatia, specifically Krajina and Eastern Slavonia. Serbia wanted to keep the Yugoslav state unified under Serb leadership. Whereas peace was established in Slovenia in June 1991 and in Croatia in January 1992, the Bosnian war escalated into a complex four year struggle that ultimately drew in the international community.

The Bosnian war is among the most complicated and intense wars since World War II. Multiple forces were involved, including paramilitary units, secret police and armed civilians supported by Bosnia, Serbia and Croatia. The ethnic groups were supported by various third parties from outside the former Yugoslav state, like the southern Slav exiles. Even the United States, with its "equip and train program" became involved. The civilian population was afflicted by ethnic rivalries. Mass deportations, detention camps and organized genocides revived memories of World War II atrocities. The war's impact on the international community was intensified by daily media reports on the heartbreaking human costs. However, involvement of Western governments was characterized by misperception and misunderstanding which delayed their engagement in the complex war until the mid-1990s. Further, despite broad agreement, the Western states differed on crucial issues and their strikingly different views inhibited coordination. The history of the Bosnian war leads naturally to questions about the essence and character of security culture.

This chapter presents the important facts and figures on the Bosnian war in the larger context of the Balkan wars overall. The complexity and intensity of the war is emphasized and major formative events are highlighted with a focus on their relevance to Germany and the U.S. The chapter ends with a brief discussion of international crisis management.

This chapter attempts to separate the inseparable in drawing a line between the major events of the Bosnian war and their reception in the Western community. Differentiating the sender and the receiver of messages is always artificial and misleading. Because the two are inextricably tied, the boundaries between them are fluid and blurred.

Thus, it is not easy to disentangle the media coverage of events in Bosnia from the reception it received in Germany and the U.S. However, differentiation is indispensable methodologically because how the events were perceived varies based on what might be called receptivity. Political reactions were strongly linked to diverging collective perceptions, which in turn were based on divergent cultural dispositions.

A.   OVERVIEW OF THE WAR

After 1989 the world underwent an unexpected political transformation. The bipolarity of the Cold War era vanished. International parameters that had guided policy for over forty years suddenly disappeared. New political actors appeared on the horizon of Europe. Interstate tensions that marked the Cold War era gave way to new, more complex intra-state crises and conflicts. These internal conflicts involve three main structural factors: weak states, intra-state security concerns and ethnic geography.[57] Another factor is the problem of "bad neighborhoods" that make weak states more vulnerable to the decisions and whims of their neighbors.[58] Small-scale conflicts can have significant spillover effects and involve whole regions, as illustrated by the wars in southeastern Europe in the late 1800's as well as the Balkan wars in the early 1900's. As in Bosnia, ethnic conflicts may involve a complex mix of cultural, ethnic, religious, regional and nationalistic causes. Nationalism in particular is a root cause of the Bos-

---

[57] Many weak states were carved out of former empires or created out of state constructs, such as Yugoslavia. They lacked political legitimacy, politically sensible borders, and political institutions capable of exercising meaningful control over the territory. Intra-state security concerns increase in those weak states when individual groups feel compelled to provide for their own safety. States with ethnic minorities are more prone to conflicts. See Michael E. Brown, "The Causes of Internal Conflict: An Overview," in *Nationalism and Ethnic Conflict*, edited by Michael E. Brown et al. (Cambridge, MA: MIT Press, 2001), 5-7.

[58] Discrete and deliberate government decisions often trigger conflicts in neighboring states for political, economic, or ideological reasons their own; see Brown, "The Causes of Internal Conflict: An Overview," 16.

nian war.[59] The Bosnian war is a stark contrast to events elsewhere in Europe, like the peaceful division of Czechoslovakia in 1993. After 1989, most of Western Europe looked for an end to confrontation, a significant peace dividend, new forms of cooperation, and above all the unification of the formerly divided continent. This mental predisposition stood in marked contrast to the downward spiral of former Yugoslavia into violent ethno-nationalism, segregation and war.[60]

After the first multiparty elections in Bosnia-Herzegovina in November 1990, the large ethnic parties formed a coalition government as a democratic alternative to the prior Socialist government. The parties organized a power sharing arrangement along ethnic lines, installing a Muslim president, a Bosnian Serb president of the parliament and a Croat prime minister. However, after Croatia and Slovenia declared independence in 1991, the Bosnian government was urged to organize a referendum for independence.[61] Voters supported independence, but the majority of Bosnian Serbs boycotted the referendum, an ominous signal of what was to come. On March 5, 1992, the Bosnian parliament declared Bosnia's independence. Full scale war broke out in Bosnia-Herzegovina. After the JNA retreated, most of its weaponry, including heavy artillery, remained in Bosnia, along with the command structure and highranking military personnel. The equipment and personnel became the backbone of the Bosnian Serb irregulars, the Army of Republika Srbska.[62]

---

[59] Stephen Van Evera identifies twenty-one hypotheses on nationalism and war; see Stephen van Evera, "Hypothesis on Nationalism and War," in Brown et al., *Nationalism and Ethnic Conflict*, 29-30. The institutional nationalism of Milosevic and Tudjman supplied the torch for the tinder of ethnic hatreds in Yugoslavia; see Warren Zimmermann quoted in Holbrooke, 24.

[60] Biermann, *Lehrjahre im Kosovo, Das Scheitern der internationalen Krisenprävention vor Kriegsausbruch*, 228.

[61] The Bosnian referendum for independence increased ethnic polarization and stood in stark contrast to the power sharing arrangements established after the multiparty elections in 1990.

[62] Jeffrey S. Lantis, *Strategic Dilemmas and the Evolution of German Foreign Policy since Unification* (Westport: Praeger Publishers, 2002), 85.

Despite inferior manpower the Bosnian Serb Army had the military advantage with heavy artillery and modern equipment.[63] Within days they gained control over regions with Serb majorities. The aim of their first strikes was to connect the five scattered Serb majority regions and unite this area with the homeland, the new Federal Republic of Yugoslavia (FRY). Within the first weeks of the war, the Army of Republika Srbska controlled over 70 percent of Bosnia-Herzegovina. Rural and urban regions came swiftly under Serb control. Exceptions were the larger cities of Sarajevo, Mostar, and Srebrenica, with their significant Muslim majorities and organized Bosnian defenses. Over a nearly-four year period, the siege of the cities varied in intensity but maintained determination to break the Bosnian forces in order to push through Serb demands. The Bosnian Serb forces encircled Sarajevo, preventing humanitarian relief convoys from entering while terrorizing and bombarding the civilians in the city.

During the long cold winter of 1992-93, the front lines were entrenched between the Bosnian Army (ARBiH) and the Army of Republika Srbska. But the Bosnian Serbs shrugged off the slow advance of their forces and exploited the increased fighting between the Croat Army (HVO) and the ARBiH. In the long siege of Mostar, the ARBiH tried to defend the city against both the Croat and the Bosnian Serb armies.

In March 1994, the U.S. and German governments brokered a peace between Croatia and Bosnia that established the Federation of Bosnia and Herzegovina, reducing the belligerents in the war to two.[64] The war continued until Croat offensives in Eastern Slavonia and Krajina drove the Serb and United Nations forces out of Western Slavonia, Smyrnia and Krajina. This was followed by the Croat attack

---

[63] Erich Rathfelder argues that the Army of Republika Srbska involved around 42,000 men in March 1992. More than 200,000 men volunteered for the Bosnian Army (ARBiH). Not all volunteers were drafted caused by the lack of weapons and ammunition; see Erich Rathfelder, "Der Krieg an seinen Schauplätzen," in: *Der Jugoslawien-Krieg Handbuch zu Vorgeschichte, Verlauf und Konsequenzen*, edited by Melcic, 353.

[64] Erich Rathfelder, "Der Krieg an seinen Schauplätzen," 360.

on Serb strongholds in Bosnia which severely tipped the balance of power on the ground and, together with NATO's operation Deliberate Force, allowed the Bosnjak-Croat Federation to gain the military initiative. Having rejected all international peace plans, the Serbs finally had to compromise.[65] Peace negotiations in Dayton, Ohio in November 1995 concluded with the signing of the General Framework Agreement for Peace in Bosnia-Herzegovina in Paris on December 14, 1995.

B.   COMPLEXITY AND INTENSITY

In the Bosnian war, issue density and issue duration were responsible for the complexity and intensity of the war as well as for its effects.[66] It was an intra-state war on the European continent, and it was ethnically motivated. Both phenomena are familiar today but were new to the policymakers of the early 1990s. In an era where nationalism, ethnicity, and war seemed part of the distant past, the sheer quantity and quality of ethnically motivated atrocity, destruction and displacement complicated the understanding of the Bosnian war. The "democratization of the means of destruction" made control of unofficial violence almost impossible.[67] The international actors' diverse historical, political and economic ties inhibited impartial judgments, and misled

---

[65] The Croat offensives in Eastern-Slavonia and the Krajina had multiple ramifications. First, they removed the myth of the invincibility of Serb forces. Second, the Croat army took the heaviest burden off NATO's shoulders by commencing the ground offensive; NATO had refrained for months from taking this last step that drew the Serbs to the negotiation table. Finally, the Croat offensive created a fait accompli for the negotiations in Dayton because compromises about Krajina and Eastern-Slavonia became obsolete. See Biermann, *Lehrjahre in Kosovo: Das Scheitern der internationalen Krisenprävention vor Kriegsausbruch*, 467-469.

[66] Celeste A. Wallander and Robert O. Keohane, "Risk, Threat, and Security Institutions," in *Imperfect Union: Security Institutions over Time and Space*, edited by Helga Haftendorn, Robert O. Keohane and Celeste A. Wallander (New York: Oxford University Press, 1999), 31-32.

[67] Eric Hobsbawm, *The Age of Extremes: A History of the World, 1914-1991* (New York: Vintage Books, 1996), 561.

and sometimes even handcuffed their crisis management activities.[68] The war itself was not the fault of the international community. It was planned and waged by Yugoslavs with "nothing to gain but everything to lose from a peaceful [state] transition."[69]

In the war, Serbia supported the Army of Republica Srpska. The Army of the Republic of Bosnia-Herzegovina, the de facto Bosnjak army, fought for an independent Bosnian state, while Croatia supported the Croat forces of Herzeg-Bosna. This led to ongoing debate over whether the conflict should be treated as a civil war or a war of aggression. Belgrade claimed the conflict was a civil war, while Croatia and the Bosnian government perceived the war as a war of aggression by Serbia. A variety of paramilitary groups were involved, supported by Serbia and Croatia and volunteers from each country. The paramilitary forces were supported by national right-wing political parties like the Serbian Radical Party. It is even alleged that Croat and Serb secret police were engaged in the conflict.

The topography of Bosnia-Herzegovina made large ground force intervention almost impossible. The mountainous terrain and virtually impassable regions made modern warfare, specifically air strikes, very difficult, but favored guerilla warfare. Memories of the war in Indochina and Vietnam scared off third party military interventions, as did the World War II myth of superior Serb fighting and guerilla war skills. Bosnia-Herzegovina's ethnic patchwork quilt made it difficult to establish a clear military front, so combined military intervention was also difficult. High losses were expected from any ground offensive. The Western community was not willing to sacrifice ground troops in combat in such an environment. Bismarck's comment that "the Balkans were not worth the bones of a single

---

[68] The Serb political leadership, and specifically the political ambitions of Milosevic, were underestimated. Milosevic was perceived as a pro-Western politician, but his political strategy was to extend his control over the Yugoslav state, compromising with critics in the wake of his radical policies. Serbia's strong nationalistic orientation was also misjudged. Thus, the belief that the Yugoslav state could solve its domestic crisis on its own reflects a failure of the Western community. See Biermann, *Lehrjahre im Kosovo: Das Scheitern der internationalen Krisenprävention vor Kriegsausbruch*, 314-319.

[69] Silber and Little, 25.

Pomeranian grenadier" echoed through parliaments and military headquarters throughout the Western community.[70]

C.   THE ROLE OF MEDIA

Satellite technology and the proliferation of networks, like Cable News Network (CNN) that present news around the clock have led to the so-called "CNN effect." Visual images have far greater power to shape perceptions than printed media and reach a broader audience. The highly competitive news industry offers images via cable to the public so quickly that pressure on politicians and foreign policy is increased.[71] The video showing a U.S. Army Ranger's body being dragged through the streets of Mogadishu had an adverse effect on the Clinton administration's willingness to stay in Somalia and derailed its 1993-1994 foreign policy agenda.[72] Once the conflict turned violent in Slovenia and Croatia, news coverage became intensive and highly emotional, featuring heartrending scenes of bloodshed that confirmed the media adage, "if it bleeds it leads."[73] The CNN effect played a crucial role in arousing public opinion, and seemed to frame the international response by seizing decisions about statecraft and the use of force from the hands of a few. United Nations Secretary General Boutros-Ghali referred to CNN as the "sixteenth member of the Security Council," saying "The member states never take action

---

[70] Christopher Cviic, *Remaking the Balkans* (New York: Council on Foreign Relations Press, 1991), 88.

[71] Margaret H. Belknap, *The CNN Effect: Strategic Enabler or Operational Risk?* (U.S. Army War College, Strategy Research Project, 2001), http://www.iwar.org.uk/psyops/resources/cnn-effect/Belknap_M_H_01.pdf, accessed 09 Apr. 2007.

[72] Steve Livingston, "'The CNN Effect': How 24-Hour News Coverage Affects Government Decisions and Public Opinion," in *A Brookings/Harvard Forum: Press Coverage and the War on Terrorism,* January 2002, http://www.brookings.edu/comm/transcripts/20020123.htm, accessed 09 Apr. 2007.

[73] Biermann, *Lehrjahre im Kosovo: Das Scheitern der internationalen Krisenprävention vor Kriegsausbruch,* 254.

on a problem unless the media take up the case."[74] Because the world was watching as the atrocities in Bosnia-Herzegovina unfolded, Western policymakers were under great pressure to respond rapidly.

Few international events after World War II had such great impact on the European and American public and political elites as the war in Bosnia. The media vied to present news and images of the mass exoduses, the death camps, ethnic cleansing, and organized rapes. Non-governmental organizations (NGOs) like Amnesty International and Human Rights Watch witnessed the atrocities in Bosnia; their reports had dramatic ramifications among international actors.[75] Western political elites who visited the Balkans returned bewildered and worried, shocked by the desperate and violent situation.[76] Western living rooms were flooded with images of atrocities like Serb onslaughts against Muslim refugees who were crowded into trucks or shot trying to escape. Seeing what Silber and Little call the "blackened skeletons of buildings [that] shape Sarajevo's skyline" caused fierce discussions in the international and domestic political debate.[77]

The Serb refugees who escaped the Croatian advance in 1995 were among the largest exoduses caused by war since the World War

---

[74] Boutros-Ghali claimed that "when the media gets involved, public opinion is aroused. Public emotion is so intense that United Nations work is undermined and constructive statesmanship is almost impossible." Bernard Kouchner, a former health minister of France and first UN governor of Kosovo from June 1999 until January 2001, is quoted as saying: "Where there is no camera, there is no humanitarian intervention." See Fred H. Cate, "'CNN effect' is Not Clear-Cut," *Humanitarian Affairs Review*, Summer 2002,
http://www.globalpolicy.org/ngos/aid/2002/summercnn.htm, accessed 09 Apr. 2007. See also Viktor Meier, "Die politische Bedeutung der Medien in der Konfliktbewaeltigung," in *Deutsche Konfliktbewaeltigung auf dem Balkan: Erfahrungen und Lehren aus dem Einsatz*, edited by Rafael Biermann (Baden-Baden: Nomos, 2002), 139-150.

[75] Amnesty International, *Concerns in Europe: July-December 1995*, Amnesty International March 1996,
http://web.amnesty.org/library/pdf/EUR010011996ENGLISH/$File/EUR01001 96.pdf, 12-14. Dorothy Q. Thomas, and E. Ralph Regan, Rape in War: Challenging the Tradition of Impunity, *SAIS Review*, 1994, 82-99,
http://www.hrw.org/women/docs/rapeinwar.htm, accessed 20 Apr. 2007.

[76] See Holbrooke's memoirs; Holbrooke, 34-54.

[77] Silber and Little, 25.

II. Half of the Bosnian population was gone, having fled or been expelled or killed. At the beginning of the war, the Bosnian Serb forces attacked the Muslim minorities in eastern Bosnia. Following the successful occupation of towns and villages, the Muslim population was captured by the military or special police forces, or was handed over by Serb civilians. Women and men were separated and isolated in detention camps. Men were generally deported, tortured or killed without trial. Women suffered unhygienic and inhumane conditions, and were mistreated and raped periodically by paramilitary units and police forces. Rape became an instrument for use in ethnic warfare.[78] Rape demoralized and humiliated the Bosnian population; it was used as a weapon with the intent of changing the ethnic demography of the whole country. Often family members were forced to watch the rapes of their beloved.[79] Eyewitness accounts and reports of refugees claimed that women were raped "everywhere and at all times, and victims [were] of all ages, from six to eighty."[80]

Muslim houses and properties were burnt down, destroyed or given to the Serb population. The Western media documented eyewitness accounts of the genocide against the Muslims of Bosnia. By June 1992 they were showing mass civilian deportations and executions in Serb military and paramilitary death camps.[81] Day after day, the media showed atrocities taking place in the middle of Europe.

Ethnic cleansing was the most common atrocity of the Bosnian war. Undesired Muslim groups were intimidated or deported from whole regions, or were killed arbitrarily. Bosnian Serb military and paramilitary units and civilians destroyed unwanted physical signs of Muslim identity like as cemeteries and places of worship. The Army of Republika Srbska slaughtered the entire civilian male population of Srebrenica, 8,000 people, within a week of occupying the city. The

---

[78] Mockaitis, 90.

[79] Karl Kaser, "Das ethnische ‚engineering‘," in: *Der Jugoslawien-Krieg Handbuch zu Vorgeschichte: Verlauf und Konsequenzen*, edited by Melcic, 418.

[80] Slavenka Drakulic, "Women Hide Behind a Wall of Silence," in *Why Bosnia? Writings on the Balkan War*, edited by Rabia Ali and Lawrence Lifschultz (Stony Creek, Connecticut: Pamphleteer's Press, 1993), 119.

[81] Mockaitis, 90.

basis of ethnic cleansing in Bosnia was not "primordial hatreds or local jealousies" but political goals.[82] The aim of ethnic cleansing, particularly in eastern Bosnia, was to terrify Muslim minorities and to force their escape into larger central enclaves like Srebrenica which were periodically attacked with heavy artillery. The overall death toll of the Bosnian war is around 102,000, including 55,000 civilians. Most fatalities were Muslim minorities in Bosnia and Herzegovina.

In sum, two factors explain the transmittance of the Bosnian war to the Western community. Formative events, like the bombing of the Sarajevo market square during the siege and the Srebrenica massacre, spurred international condemnation. Second and equally striking was the effect of the war as a whole. The issue density of single atrocities along with the issue duration of the war attracted the press and media.

D. INTERNATIONAL CRISIS MANAGEMENT

What the publics in Europe remember from the Bosnian war is the sense of political impotence that surrounded the handling of the crisis. The western governments and the UN sought a diplomatic solution while conducting a peacekeeping mission (UNPROFOR) in an escalating conflict and humanitarian nightmare. A classical UN peacekeeping operation, authorized during an unfolding war, tried not to solve but to contain the conflict, i.e. to alleviate human suffering and avert spill-over into the neighborhood. In other words, "the problem in Yugoslavia was not how to police a peace but rather how to establish one."[83]

---

[82] Gagnon argues that a violent conflict is not caused by ethnic sentiments, but rather by the dynamics of in-group conflicts. Thus, a conflict along ethnic cleavages is provoked by elites to create a domestic political context within which ethnicity is the only politically relevant identity. In the Yugoslav case, ethnic hatreds were not the central cause of the conflict. See V.P. Gagnon, Jr., "Ethnic Nationalism and International Conflict: The Case of Serbia," *International Security* 19, no. 3 (Winter 1994/95), 131-134; see also Woodward, 242.

[83] Jonathan Eyal, *Europe and Yugoslavia: Lessons from a Failure* (London: Royal United Services for Defence Studies, 1993), 79.

36

Early misperceptions hindered an effective response. American warnings of an outbreak of war channeled through NATO were "muted" by the European Community. [84] Silence reigned on the diplomatic front prior to April 1991, partly due to misperceptions of the forces in Yugoslavia.[85]

Paradoxically, the outbreak of the war caught the European Community by surprise, whether knowingly or unknowingly. Its reaction was hasty and overambitious, caused by uncertainty and a misperception of the conflict. In June 1991, the Dutch Foreign Minister, Hans van den Broek, declared the crisis on the Balkans to be a European matter, saying "We do not interfere in American affairs; we trust America will not interfere in European affairs."[86] Washington would be kept informed but not consulted, according to Gianni de Michelis, Foreign Minister of Italy. The U.S. was more than happy to retreat after the visit of Secretary of State James Baker to Belgrade in June 1991 and the first Iraq war. While eyes focused on the Persian Gulf, the Bush administration was also committed to the Yugoslav status quo as means to prevent the break up of the Soviet Union and generalized chaos in Europe.

A variety of different trans-Atlantic organizations were involved in the crisis management. The self-confident claim that Balkan wars are European business and that the EC would refuse involvement by other organizations and states demobilized the United States and thus NATO.[87] The EC misperceived the Yugoslav War as a manageable crisis, especially after the initial success of the Brioni agreement for Slovenia. The United Nations, also first successful with

---

84 Rafael Biermann, "Back to the Roots: The European Community and the Dissolution of Yugoslavia – Policies under the Impact of Global Sea-Change," *Journal of European Integration History* 10, no. 1 (2004), 48.

85 Biermann, "Back to the Roots: The European Community and the Dissolution of Yugoslavia – Policies under the Impact of Global Sea-Change," 36.

86 Jacques Delors, President of the European Community, cited in Holbrooke, 21.

87 The President of the European Council, Jacques Poos, claimed in 1991 that the Balkan wars are the "hour of Europe. If one problem can be solved by the Europeans, it is the Yugoslav problem. This is a European country and it is not up to the Americans. It is not up to anyone else;" see Almond, 32.

ending the war in Croatia (Vance Plan), was soon overwhelmed by the war's complexity and unable to deploy effective ad hoc military forces. With the Security Council unwilling to equip UN units with peace enforcing mandates, the UN maneuvered itself into a deadlock. The Protection Force of the United Nations (UNPROFOR) had a mandate to prevent conflict and was specifically equipped for that mission. Neither the armaments nor the mandate itself were sufficient to enforce peace between the belligerents. As a whole, UNPROFOR could not stop the war; it "lacked the firepower to halt the fighting and stop the slaughter."[88] Thus the UN was confined to damage limitation and engaged in no full-fledged conflict resolution.[89] The consensus-based CSCE likewise proved incapable of halting the atrocities. Early diplomatic efforts by the EC and CSCE assumed a functioning, undivided Yugoslav state.[90] Different institutions were focused on their respective areas of responsibility with little cooperation among them. With Europe still preoccupied with internal transformation, what was needed to manage a complex crisis, the concept of "interlocking institutions," simply did not exist.[91] That said, international involvement also lacked effective, goal oriented cooperation.

Various plans for peace were drawn up throughout the Balkan war.[92] The London Conference in August 1992 outlined broad principles to end the war. The international actors agreed to establish the International Conference on Former Yugoslavia (ICFY) as a permanent bargaining forum co-chaired by the EC (David Owen, later Carl Bildt) and the UN (Special Envoy Cyrus Vance, followed by Thorvald Stoltenberg).[93] The ICFY declared Serb forces the main aggressor, threatened the use of military force, and insisted that international

---

[88] Mockaitis, 91.

[89] Bennett, 236.

[90] Woodward, 379.

[91] Biermann, *Lehrjahre im Kosovo, Das Scheitern der internationalen Krisenprävention vor Kriegsausbruch*, 83.

[92] The most significant peace plans and forums were the International Conference on Former Yugoslavia (ICFY), the Vance-Owen Plan and the Dayton Peace Accord.

[93] Mockaitis, 98-99.

borders be recognized in the conflict. It proved an effective forum for coordinated diplomatic responses to the war, and it presented the first plans to end the war in Bosnia, the Vance-Owen Plan.[94] However, the Vance-Owen Plan, which originated in "efforts to reduce friction among international actors,"[95] could be rejected by the Bosnian Serb parliament in Pale because of internal divisions in the West, and specifically because it was rejected by the Clinton administration.[96] The later Owen-Stoltenberg Plan likewise failed.

Overall, more than thirty countries and their armed forces, coordinated by the UN, NATO, and WEU, were involved in the peace keeping effort. They carried out six different missions established by UN Resolutions.[97] The complexity of the military intervention required strict coordination and an agreed framework for civil-military cooperation, neither of which existed in the first years of the Bosnian war.[98]

The growing understanding of the importance of a coherent international diplomatic effort and specifically of the "need to harmonize policy" led to the creation of the Contact Group in early 1994.[99] German diplomatic efforts encouraged Russia to participate in the forum. The Contact Group was created to facilitate coordination among the U.S., Russia, Germany, France and Great Britain, to "formulate a coherent strategy in Bosnia," and to diminish the differences among the main actors.[100] It followed a hard and consistent line

---

[94] The plan proposed the partition of Bosnia into nine provinces, three ruled by Serbs, one by Croats and five by Muslim and Croats.

[95] Gow, 223.

[96] The U.S. was not willing to accept a commitment to be prepared to implement the Vance-Owen Plan even partly; see Gow, 258.

[97] Gow, 129.

[98] Gow argues that peacekeeping is an element of peace support, which in Clausewitzian terms is "continuation of policy by other means." Peace support denotes military operations under the primary purpose of international diplomacy; see Gow, 127.

[99] Gow, 156.

[100] Mockaitis, 104.

of negotiations, setting up the Contact Group Peace Plan.[101] Whereas the Contact Group acted as a forum for the great powers, it also demonstrated the necessity of coordination among international organizations.[102] Led by NATO, and thus the U.S., the Contact Group sidelined the UN and the EU whose diplomatic efforts were long exhausted. In the fall of 1995, NATO finally acted to enforce peace in the war-shattered Bosnia with effective and resolute military engagement backed by coordinated diplomacy.

Four years of the worst fighting in post-World War II Europe thus ended in precisely the way the Western Alliance had said it could not end: NATO enforced peace by attacking the major aggressor.[103] Early international actions had benefited the Serbs and Croats and, by definition, hurt the Bosnjaks. Permanent aggression by the Republica Srbska Forces was obscured by the international decision to claim a neutral position early in the conflict by designating all belligerents in the conflict as responsible.[104] It took extensive NATO air strikes and 60.000 heavy armed combat troops to make and keep the peace in Bosnia and Herzegovina.

E.   CONCLUSION

The international community took almost four years to stop the slaughter in Bosnia and Herzegovina. There are many reasons why the international organizations and their principals were reluctant to intervene in a forceful and coordinated fashion. There were many disagreements among on how to handle the crisis. The European states had more in common with one another than with the United States.[105] This was obvious with European efforts to involve Russia and to maintain a strict arms embargo, in contrast to American efforts

---

[101] The peace plan was a "take it or leave it" proposition, with rewards when it was followed and punishments when it was ignored.

[102] Christoph Schwegmann, *The Contact Group and its Impact on the European Institutional Structure*, 8.

[103] Mockaitis, 116.

[104] Mockaitis, 94.

[105] Gow, 182.

to tip the military balance in favor of the perceived victims, the Bosnjaks. They did share reluctance to send ground troops into combat, a desire to alleviate the impact of the war, and the aspiration to work multilaterally. However, the multilateral approach suffered from lack of effective cooperation and coordination.

Multiple misperceptions led to unenthusiastic crisis management focused on diplomacy. Uncertainties and instability hindered strong and coherent attention to crisis prevention and conflict resolution. The complexity and intensity of the war in Bosnia deterred international action. Historical and economic ties inhibited impartial intervention and tied the hands of the states involved. The atrocities and the fighting during the Bosnian war made understanding the conflict complicated; in the early years, most international actors closed their eyes to the atrocities against the Bosnjaks. On the other hand, the humanitarian nightmare spurred rethinking and oriented the international community towards more effective intervention. Reunited Europe's enthusiasm contrasts dramatically with the violence of the Bosnian war. From the European perspective, it was unthinkable that nationalism and ethnic warfare, banished since 1945, would arise again on European soil.

IV.   GERMAN SECURITY CULTURE TRANS-FORMED

In an interview on February 7, 1992, German Chancellor Helmut Kohl said, "Germans should not be the first to stick their neck out. One will not be overlooked even if one remains a bit more in the background."[106] This reflects the traditional "culture of restraint" that has dominated German foreign and security policy since 1949 and had just been affirmed by the German refusal to contribute troops to the UN-mandated international coalition to force Iraq back out of Kuwait. In March, fierce attacks in eastern and northwestern Bosnia ushered in one of the most violent and destructive conflicts since the Second World War. The subsequent three years of war would have a profound impact on German security culture. Almost four years later, in a parliamentary speech on December 6, 1995, Kohl declared that "the international community's expectations of unified Germany are different from those placed upon the old Federal Republic." Germany today, he said, "must stand alongside them in preserving peace," adding that Germany "must not and can not withdraw from such a mis-

---

[106] Kohl quoted in Lantis, "The Moral Imperative of Force: The Evolution of German Strategic Culture in Kosovo," *Comparative Strategy* 21, (2002), 21. On German security culture, this author relied on following works: Donald Abenheim, *Soldiers and Politics Transformed: German-American Reflections on Civil-Military Relations in a New Strategic Environment* (Berlin: Carole Hartmann Miles-Verlag, 2006); Bundesministerium der Verteidigung, *Weißbuch 1994: Weißbuch zur Sicherheit der Bundesrepublik Deutschland und zur Lage und Zukunft der Bundeswehr,* Bundesministerium der Verteidigung im Auftrag der Bundesregierung, 1994; John S. Duffield, *World Power Forsaken: Political Culture, International Institutions and German Security Policy After Unification* (Stanford: Stanford University Press, 1998); Helga Haftendorn, *Deutsche Aussenpolitik zwischen Selbstbeschränkung und Selbstbehauptung 1945-2000* (Muenchen: Deutsche Verlagsanstalt, 2001); Wolfram Hilz, *Europas verhindertes Führungstrio: Die Sicherheitspolitik Deutschlands, Frankreichs und Großbritanniens in den Neunzigern* (Paderborn: Ferdinand Schöningh, 2005); Karl Kaiser and Hans W. Maull, eds., *Deutschlands neue Außenpolitik: Band 1: Grundlagen* (München: Oldenburg, 1994); Jeffrey S. Lantis, *Strategic Dilemmas and the Evolution of German Foreign Policy since Unification* (Westport: Praeger Publishers, 2002); Jeffrey S. Lantis, "The Moral Imperative of Force: The Evolution of German Strategic Culture in Kosovo;" Max Otte, *A Rising Middle Power? German Foreign Policy in Transformation, 1989-1999* (New York: St. Martin's Press, 2000).

sion."[107] Eight days later the signing of the Dayton Peace Accords ended the cruel, ferocious and complex war in Bosnia, and Germany for the first time contributed its Bundeswehr to an international peace building operation. The Bosnian war was a political shock experience with far-ranging repercussions for German society and political elites. Germany's security culture, which until 1992 did not recognize the legitimacy of employing German forces for foreign policy reasons other than national and collective defense, was transformed by the war.

The Bosnian war presented Germany with a challenge (perceived by some as an opportunity) to reshape its foreign policy by assuming more responsibility in international affairs. This became visible in regard to the culture of restraint that had guided German international activities throughout the Cold War. With the Bosnian war in Europe's backyard, German society and political leadership were caught in a strategic dilemma between humanitarianism and history, between "Idealpolitik" and "Realpolitik," which required rethinking security and military policy. The core elements of German foreign policy had overall remained intact after reunification. Since there was no break with the past, German foreign policy had a high degree of continuity and moderation, and the political culture adjusted slowly to the new responsibilities of an enlarged Germany. The changing international environment, specifically the Bosnian war experience, accelerated changes in the traditional security culture that was increasingly at odds with the post-Cold War reality.

A.   GERMAN HISTORY AND FOREIGN POLICY PREDISPOSITIONS

This section examines the sources and development of German security culture after World War II, emphasizing the rationale for Germany's cultural preferences and explaining the cultural predispositions of the German public and political elites.

---

107 Lantis, *Strategic Dilemmas and the Evolution of German Foreign Policy since Unification*, 130.

Germany's long and varied history and its "past transgressions"[108] have long lasting ramifications on its foreign policy. As the aggressor in both world wars and perpetrator of "made in Germany" violence, atrocities, slaughter, and genocide during national socialist rule, Germans have long been perceived by their critics as by nature "subservient to authority, militaristic, and aggressive."[109] After World War II, European neighbors perceived a defeated Germany as "a mutable, Proteuslike, unpredictable country, particularly dangerous when it is unhappy."[110] "Incertitudes Allemagne," a standard phrase in France throughout the Cold War, was revived again during German unification. Those historically conditioned attitudes constrained West Germany's foreign policy, as did the Soviet ideological and military threat, the dependence on the United States for security, and the partition into West and East. Those constraints were intensified by being geostrategically positioned in the "Mittellage"[111] between U.S.-NATO and USSR-Warsaw Pact. Desiring both strong Western ties and a foreign policy that would not antagonize the Soviet Union, West Germany was stuck in a strategic dilemma. The subject of East Germany exceeds the scope of this study and has been treated elsewhere.[112]

Thus, Germany had no desire to flex its muscles with the kind of nation-state independence often demonstrated by France and especially the United States. Or the Federal Republic of Germany (FRG) did so in a manner that was barely perceptible as muscle flexing, even when in fact it was, e.g. Willy Brandt's Ostpolitik in the early

---

108 Duffield, 43.

109 Gordon A. Craig, *The Politics of the Prussian Army 1640-1945* (New York: Oxford University Press, 1955), xiii.

110 Luigi Barzini, *The Europeans* (New York: Simon and Schuster, 1983), 267.

111 Helga Haftendorn, "Gulliver in der Mitte Europas: Internationale Verflechtung und nationale Handlungsmöglichkeiten," in: *Deutschlands neue Außenpolitik. Band 1: Grundlagen*, edited by Karl Kaiser and Hans W. Maull, (München: Oldenbourg, 1994).

112 For East German foreign policy see Joachim Scholtyseck, *Die Außenpolitik der DDR* (München: Oldenbourg Wissenschaftsverlag, 2003), Hans Adolf Jacobsen, *Drei Jahrzehnte Assenpolitik der DDR: Bestimmungsfaktoren, Instrumente, Aktionsfelder* (München: Oldenbourg Verlag, 1979), and Kurt Sontheimer and Wilhelm Bleek, *Die DDR: Politik Gesellschaft, Wirtschaft* (Hamburg: Hoffmann und Kampe, 1979).

1970s or Helmut Schmidt's call for missiles in 1977. Konrad Adenauer, the first post-war German Chancellor, had already formulated the principle guidelines of German post-War foreign policy. The essence was an extraordinary focus on multilateral diplomacy within international institutions and integration into the European project. Thus, Germany could gain new prestige and leverage in world affairs without arousing its suspicious war-time enemies and new friends. In fact, soon Germans perceived this stress on multilateralism as the only legitimate way to global peace. Adenauer adopted a completely Western-oriented foreign policy, dubbed "Westbindung." In the Grand Coalition of 1966-69, Foreign Minister Hans Dietrich Genscher (1974-1992) developed what he called "Verantwortungspolitik," a foreign policy of responsibility, "oriented around the themes of restraint, humanitarianism and multilateral cooperation."[113] Later this policy orientation was dubbed "Genscherism," with some pejorative, ironic undertones, especially in the United States. German foreign and security culture was based on a "Kultur der Zurückhaltung," culture of restraint, a term also coined by Genscher and accepted by his successor Klaus Kinkel. This culture of restraint focused on diplomacy and was strongly skeptical about the use of force, renouncing the use of any military force beyond the collective defense obligation of NATO. This was based on a consensual reading of the German Basic Law up to the 1990s. Harnessed multilaterally, by 1990 Germany had rehabilitated itself within international institutions and became the strongest advocate of European integration, participating in the Common Market, Political Union and European Political Cooperation, and as a recognized member of NATO and the United Nations.

In sum, German foreign and security policy was exceptional and radically different from that of other countries in Europe especially that of the UK and France.[114] German exceptionalism is based on the unique national security culture that developed in response to the fallacies of Hitler's Germany. Germany was perceived as a reluctant power, a pressured power, definitely as a civilian power (despite the fighting power of the Bundeswehr by the 1980s), and as a *World*

---

113 Lantis, "The Moral Imperative of Force," 22.

114 Hilz, 44.

power forsaken.[115] During the Cold War, Germany pursued its national interests in a non-threatening and low-profile way based on the culture of restraint.[116]

The "new world order," a term coined at the end of the First World War, predicted a new period of history with dramatic changes in political thought and the balance of power. The unexpected decline of the Soviet Empire involved the world in a similarly dramatic political transformation. This new world order harnessed new concepts and expectations, such as the replacement of containment with superpower cooperation. This cooperation among a new, more unified Europe could focus on reducing armaments and troop deployments, settling regional disputes, stimulating economic growth, diffusing democratic governance, lessening East-West trade restrictions, spreading humanitarianism and protecting the environment. In this context, German foreign policy culture seemed perfectly prepared. In Europe, German reunification was seen as part of this new world order.

It was hoped that the new world order would be based on principles of political liberty, self-determination, non-intervention and integration and would refrain from using military force, which was viewed as a threat by many in Germany. The ideals of the new world order help to explain the weak German reaction at the outbreak of the Bosnian war.

After reunification in 1990, Germany was expected to respond more independently, freed from the handcuffs of history, especially in regard to the deployment of its armed forces in multilateral peacekeeping efforts. One should keep in mind that the Kuwait annexation of August 1990 unfolded just as the "two-plus-four negotiations" on German unification were coming to a climax. Lantis notes: "Neorealists predicted that the Federal Republic would soon 'normal-

---

[115] Multiple scholars of international relations have studied German exceptionalism and came to similar conclusions; see Thomas Kielinger and Max Otte, "Germany-The Pressured Power," *Foreign Policy* 91, no.2 (1993), 44-62; Hanns Maull, "Zivilmacht Bundesrepublik: Vierzehn Thesen für eine neue deutsche Aussenpolitik," *Europa-Archiv* 47, no.1 (1992), 269-278; Duffield.

[116] The non-threatening and low-profile approach is described in Hilz, 45.

ize' its foreign policy by taking on a more assertive foreign profile focused on strategic interests, backed by the threat of the use of force."[117] The leading figure of this school, John Mearsheimer, flatly predicted that Germany would seek nuclear weapons.[118] Germany's foreign policy was indeed changing since 1989. The way the Kohl government conducted—perhaps even dominated—the German internal unification process as well as the "two-plus-four negotiations," went beyond the culture of restraint. Also, the manner in which Germany imposed its will on its European partners concerning recognition of Croatia and Slovenia seemed to signal a new German assertiveness on the diplomatic front. Militarily, German security policy was more cautious, yet also slowly transforming. Germany supported the operation in the Persian Gulf in 1991 financially and provided logistical support to Turkey and Israel; further it contributed military forces to the UN operations in Cambodia and Somalia in 1993, and it strongly advocated diplomatic recognition of Croatia and Slovenia in 1991.[119] But the traditional political norms and values limited German participation in international crisis management in the early phase of this national realignment of diplomacy and strategy. Public opinion was hostile to German military power and the use of force which was seen in exclusively tragic terms. Germany was reluctant to contribute its Bundeswehr to international operations, even if UN mandated, and at the same time lacked the will actively to oppose the interventions of the traditional powers. The political leadership refused to support Operation Desert Storm with German forces because of the still unchallenged domestic political consensus that the German Basic Law, especially Article 87a, prohibited using military force outside

---

[117] Lantis, "The Moral Imperative of Force," 23.

[118] John J. Mearsheimer, "Back to the Future: Instability in Europe after the Cold War" *International Security* 15, no. 1 (Summer 1990), 5-56.

[119] Lantis, *Strategic Dilemmas and the Evolution of German Foreign Policy since Unification*, 10, 17-38.

NATO territory. The consensus among parties as well as lawyers was that Germany should stick to its traditional political boundaries.[120]

Germany had built strong economic ties and a special relationship with Yugoslavia during the Cold War if not before when one considers the Habsburg legacy. As Yugoslavia's largest trading partner, Germany took the lead in rescheduling the debts of the Balkan republic.[121] The strong social and economic relationship was evident in the hundreds of thousands of guest workers in Germany, the German tourists at the Adriatic coast, and numerous city partnerships.[122] Germany was a strong advocate that Yugoslavia be among the first to sign an association agreement with the European Community and the Visegrad countries in 1990. During the outbreak of the Balkan war in 1991 the EC still signed the third financial protocol with Yugoslavia to extend credits. Fifty years earlier, in April 1941, German ties with the Balkan had been of a different, tragic kind. Germany became involved "directly in Balkan affairs... when Hitler ordered the invasion and occupation of the region."[123] After only eleven days, Yugoslavia surrendered unconditionally. The German forces were supported by radical Croat nationalists, the Ustashes, in their struggle against mainly Serb nationalistic groups, called Chetniks, and Communist parti-

---

[120] Lantis, "The Moral Imperative of Force," 26. For detailed information see Nina Philippi, *Bundeswehr-Auslandseinsaetze als aussen- und sicherheitspolitisches Problem des geeinten Deutschland* (Frankfurt a.M.: Peter Lang Publishing Inc., 1997) and Alexander Siedschlag, *Die aktive Beteiligung Deutschlands an miliaerischen Aktionen zur Verwirklichung Kollektiver Sicherheit* (Frankfurt a.M.: Peter Lang Publishing Inc., 1995).

[121] Rafael Biermann, "Back to the Roots: The European Community and the Dissolution of Yugoslavia – Policies under the Impact of Global Sea-Change," 38.

[122] Hilz, 245-246.

[123] Lantis, *Strategic Dilemmas and the Evolution of German Foreign Policy since Unification*, 80. For World War II on the Balkans see Andrew L. Zapantis, *Hitler's Balkan Campaign and the Invasion of the USSR* (New York: Columbia University Press, 1987); Walter Ansel, *Hitler and the Middle Sea* (Durham, N.C.: Duke University Press, 1972); Rainer Mennel, *Der Balkan: Einfluss und Interessensphaeren* (Osnabrueck: Biblio Verlag, 1999).

sans.[124] Italians and Germans created the only Greater Albania in history to counterbalance the Serb resistance. Germany thus ushered in the civil war in Yugoslavia which cost millions of lives until the Germans withdrew in 1944. This was still in the mind of policymakers like Helmut Kohl, who in the early 1990s urged restraint in German Balkan policy in the early 1990s.

Still, the Balkan war increasingly challenged German security culture and triggered a fundamental reorientation of its foreign policy.[125] First, reunited Germany had to redefine its national foreign policy aims, including its relation to international partners within the Euro- and Transatlantic alliances and organizations. Second, reunited Germany had to decide whether it was able and willing to carry more responsibility in international crisis management, specifically military responsibility. This clearly was expected by its partners, who during the first Gulf War heavily criticized the German policy of "Scheckbuchdiplomatie," paying of war expenses without contributing forces. The reorientation process had a direct impact on German foreign policy at the outbreak of the Balkan wars. Domestic problems associated with foreign policy transformation were not resolved in 1991, and Germany's focus was thus more internal than external.

In sum, modern German history accounts for its singular foreign policy during the Cold War. Germany was restrained by its own past and by the international environment, which saw Germany as a potential threat and as an ally against Soviet imperialism. German foreign policy was pursuing international rehabilitation through integration and cooperation, rather than purely national interests and objectives by power politics alone. During the Cold War, Germany developed a unique "military strategic culture" which included a large mili-

---

124 Lantis, *Strategic Dilemmas and the Evolution of German Foreign Policy since Unification*, 80. For German operations in the Balkans in World War II, see Center on Military History, *German Antiguerilla Operations in the Balkans (1941-1944)*, (Washington D.C.: U.S. Government Printing Office, 1989); Ronald H. Bailey *Partisans and Guerillas* (Alexandria, Va.: Time-Life Books, 1978); Misha Glenny, *The Balkans: Nationalism, War, and the Great Powers, 1804-1999* (New York: Viking, 2000); Jozo Tomasevich, *War and Revolution in Yugoslavia: Occupation and Collaboration, 1941-1945* (Stanford: Stanford University Press, 2001).

125 Hilz, 243.

tary force to bear its burden of territorial defense within treaty obligations, but refused to participate in any out-of-area operations which were seen as neo-imperialist undertakings.[126] Thus restrictions on the use of military force "became deeply rooted in the public psyche."[127] The strict interpretation of the Basic Law served this purpose. After reunification, the internal and external conditions changed and German political and security culture became less homogeneous. Lantis writes, a "new consensus emerged among American scholars that Germany's political culture of reticence—not systemic characteristics—would define its foreign affairs profile."[128] They claimed that explaining German security policy development required using concepts such as political and security culture.

B. GERMAN PREDISPOSITIONS AND EARLY PERCEPTIONS OF THE WAR

Because the first signs of cultural changes were visible prior the outbreak of the Bosnian war, this section guides the reader through the early Balkan wars, examines the early German perception of the Bosnian war, and analyzes the impact of the wars in Croatia and Slovenia on German predispositions. A certain amount of overlap in the subsequent discussion cannot be avoided because the relevant predispositions of the German public and political elites are closely interrelated.

The German foreign policy emphasis on responsibility and the culture of restraint is responsible for German public and elite predispositions and thus for their perceptions at the outbreak of the Bosnian war. Along with domestic predispositions, changing events in the new international environment and economic and social ties with the Yugoslav state explain the complexity of Germans' early views.

---

[126] Hilz, 45.

[127] Lantis, "The Moral Imperative of Force," 22.

[128] Lantis, "The Moral Imperative of Force," 23.

1. Predispositions and Perceptions Caused by German Domestic Policy

The outbreak of the war in 1991 caused fierce discussions between the government and the opposition and within the political parties themselves. The war affected the German government and society almost immediately.[129] Within a few weeks, about 20,000 refugees sought asylum in Germany, a figure which increased to 180,000 by the end of 1992.[130] Germany gave asylum to 350,000 refugees from former Yugoslavia until 1995. The Bosnian war threatened to spill over to the former Yugoslav republics and provinces, especially to Macedonia, Kosovo and Sandzak, and further across the borders of former Yugoslavia into Albania, Bulgaria and Greece with their Serb and Muslim minorities. That would have involved NATO territory. While 54 percent of Germans thought that the war would remain isolated in the Balkans, 28 percent felt that the war might threaten overall European security.[131] German politicians, listening to the rising public outrage in the larger capitals, negotiated for months on how to stop the war atrocities.

The major domestic political debate focused on the constitutionality of German military forces being deployed in UN peacekeeping and NATO out-of-area missions.[132] Because of Tito's split from

---

[129] Lantis, *Strategic Dilemmas and the Evolution of German Foreign Policy since Unification*, 82

[130] Haftendorn, *Deutsche Aussenpolitik zwischen Selbstbeschraenkung und Selbstbehauptung 1945-2000*, 410.

[131] Lantis, *Strategic Dilemmas and the Evolution of German Foreign Policy since Unification*, 85.

[132] Karin Johnston, "German Public Opinion and the Crisis in Bosnia," in *International Public Opinion and the Bosnia Crisis,* edited by Richard Sobel and Eric Shiraev (New York: Lexington Books, 2003), 269. There was a lack of coherent rules in the Basic Law concerning the use of German forces. Domestically the most important reason for the omission of those rules was the disagreement between the main political parties in 1949. Thus, the future military role of the Federal Republic was and remained unresolved. See Georg Nolte, "Germany: Ensuring Political Legitimacy for the Use of Military Forces by Requiring Constitutional Accountability," in *Democratic Accountability and the Use of Force in International Law*, edited by Charlotte Ku and Harold K. Jacobsen (New York: Cambridge University Press, 2002), 232.

the communist Soviet Union in 1948, the German Social Democrat Party (SPD) had a strong affinity to the Yugoslav state and thus hesitated to use force against Serb aggression. Furthermore, toward the end of the Cold War, the SPD had become strongly averse to the use of combat via military force, partly due to the myth that any military entanglement would endanger the fruits of the former "Ostpolitik."[133] It was seen as having "potentially serious reverberations in [the] relationship with the Soviet Union and Eastern Europe."[134] This notion became internalized by all German political elites.

In 1981, the government formed by the SPD and the German Liberal Party (FDP) took the position that a combat use of the Bundeswehr outside NATO territory was unconstitutional. Former Chancellor Helmut Schmidt and Foreign Minister Hans Dietrich Genscher accepted this interpretation, although "[t]here was, however, no consensus among constitutional scholars that such a restriction, in fact, existed."[135] The original clause in the Basic Law (Article 24) allowed the federal government to enter into a system of mutual collective security to maintain peace. The amendment of the mid-1950s, Article 87(a), added that the use of German forces was only allowed for national defense.[136] Thus, there was an inherent tension between the articles. While the Christian Democratic Party (CDU) and the Christian Social Party (CSU) focused on Article 24, the SPD upheld to the narrower interpretation of Article 87(a), rejecting any military en-

---

[133] "Ostpolitik" describes a policy of rapprochement towards the Soviet Union and Central Eastern Europe, and specifically towards the German Democratic Republik (GDR), in order to normalize international relations with the region. It was first coined by Egon Bahr in 1963 and articulated as the main political aim during the chancellorship of Willy Brandt. It was not diametrically opposed to the former policy of "Westbindung" articulated by Konrad Adenauer, but was pursued by the Federal Republic of Germany to bridge the antagonism of the "Mittellage," and to normalize and ease relationships between the two Germanys.

[134] Johnston, 270.

[135] Johnston, 270.

[136] Article 87(a) had been amended to incorporate a domestic emergency role. In 1968 the Federal Republic was not yet a member of the UN, and so no one considered the possibility of German forces participating in UN peacekeeping operations. See Nolte, 236.

gagement beyond NATO collective defense, including UN peace-keeping.[137] In 1991, the CDU and the CSU, together with the FDP and the SPD, agreed on the need for a constitutional amendment to clarify the issue. But whereas the CDU and CSU advocated a broader interpretation concerning the use of force, the SPD insisted on a more narrow range of options. The dispute stalled the negotiations on the amendment.

Within the SPD, aversion to military force became deeply rooted in party politics that had already been driven to extremes by the Intermediate Nuclear Forces Crisis of the early 1980s and the rise of the Greens. The party manifesto of the SPD, known as the "Berliner Programm,"[138] focused on social equality, adjustment of the economy, ecology, and most importantly, peace politics. The manifesto stated that German armed forces were to be employed solely to defend German territory.[139] Further, it stated that peace politics diminish the utility of the military as an instrument of policy overall.

In June 1991, Kohl urged the German political parties "to participate in negotiations to restore the Yugoslav federation."[140] But strong emotional reactions and debate over Germany's own reunification demanded another course of action. Pressure from German society[141] and interest groups of Yugoslavian guest workers,[142] along with

---

[137] Johnston, 271.

[138] The Berliner Programm was the general program of the Social Democrat Party in 1989.

[139] It should be mentioned that the statements in the manifesto did not display the thinking of a strong majority of the party. That said, a majority of social democratic elites saw the mutual collective defense within NATO as necessary and right and therefore also supported the deployment of German troops outside the national territory to meet treaty obligations. Grundsatzprogramm der Sozialdemokratischen Partei Deutschlands," 16, http://www.spd-schleswig-holstein.de/docs /1118733935_programmdebatte_grundsatzprogramm.pdf, accessed 12.Feb. 2007.

[140] Lantis, *Strategic Dilemmas and the Evolution of German Foreign Policy since Unification*, 83.

[141] The CSU representatives accused Chancellor Kohl of supporting the communists in Serbia while not recognizing Croatia and Slovenia; see James Gow, *Triumph of the Lack of Will, International Diplomacy and the Yugoslav War* (New York: Columbia University Press, 1997), 167.

the bias against military force and the will to internationalize of the conflict, drove Kohl and Genscher to early diplomatic recognition of Croatia and Slovenia. Together with other prevailing circumstances, the possibility of combat and involving German troops in an escalating conflict persuaded them "to pursue the diplomatic route of recognition."[143] Public opinion perceived a strong contrast between domestic events and the international environment. While Germany grew larger with peaceful reunification, Eastern and South Eastern Europe turned towards disintegration and dissolution of the order stipulated in the Paris suburb treaties of 1919.[144] Paradoxically, the reunification of Germany and the dissolution of Yugoslavia were based on the same rationale: the right of national self determination.[145] Thus the reunited Germany favored negotiations and recognition of Slovenia and Croatia while other European countries and the UN favored only a negotiated settlement.[146] All German parties sup-

[142] More than 600,000, of the 750,000 Yugoslavian permanent guest workers were of direct Croat descent. This interest group favored Christian democrat partisanship and lobbied for early recognition in the German government; see Lantis, *Strategic Dilemmas and the Evolution of German Foreign Policy since Unification*, 85.

[143] Lantis , *Strategic Dilemmas and the Evolution of German Foreign Policy since Unification*, 84; For the different elements of German attitudes which persuaded the political elites to pursue the diplomatic route of recognition, see Michael Libal, "The Road to Recognition: Germany, the EC and the Disintegration of Yugoslavia 1991," in *Journal of European Integration History* 10, no.1 (Baden-Baden: Nomos Verlagsgesellschaft, 2004) 77.

[144] Robert H. Dorff, "German Policy Toward Peace Support Operations," *Force, Statecraft and German Unity: The Struggle to Adapt Institutions and Practices*, Strategic Studies Institute, US Army War College, Carlisle Barracks, PA. December 1996, 64.

[145] Bruno Schoch, "Anerkennen als Ersatzhandlung / Ein kritischer Rückblick auf die Bonner Jugoslawienpolitik," in: *Der Krieg in Bosnien das hilflose Europa / Plädoyer für eine militärissche UN-Intervention*, (Frankfurt aM: Hessische Stiftung Friedens- und Konfliktforschung (Hrsg.), 1993), 38.

[146] Hans-Ulrich Seidt, "Führung in der Krise? Die Balkankriege und das Deutsche Konfliktmanagement, " in: *Deutsche Konfliktbewältigung auf dem Balkan: Erfahrunden und Lehren aus dem Einsatz*, edited by Rafael Biermann (Baden-Baden: Nomos Verlagsgesellschaft, 2002), 40-42.

ported the diplomatic route of early recognition.[147] Even the chief foreign policy spokesman of the SPD, Norbert Gansel, confirmed after visiting the Balkans that recognizing independent states would be more effective than a policy of pressure.[148] The German effort to recognize Croatia and Slovenia early was based on the fact that "German leaders were more willing than other Europeans to verify Serbia as the aggressor in this conflict"[149] and to see the others as victims. The German government did not see that recognizing the former Yugoslavian republics was a one-shot weapon. Nevertheless, in early 1992 other European states followed the German example of recognizing Croatia and Slovenia. Even the strongest advocate of Yugoslav integrity, the U.S., pursued this diplomatic course of action.

Germany's strong economic and political relationship with Yugoslavia was specifically oriented towards Croatia, as most Yugoslav guest workers were of Croat descent. This perceived relationship was "vindicated by the relentless pursuit of conquest and ethnic cleansing by the Serbs."[150] This does not imply that the nationalistic policy of Tudjman's Croatia was neglected by the German government. The Serb attack on the Croat city Dubrovnik, an Adriatic attraction for thousands of German tourists and a World Cultural Heritage site, revived memories of the German conquest in World War II, as did the brutal attack on Vukovar.[151] However, aspirations for a "Greater Croatia" were not accepted by Germany.[152]

---

[147] The Politbarometer survey in fall 1991 revealed that almost 78 percent of all German supported the Croatian and Slovenian independence attempt; see Johnston, 260. Other institutes claim that 84 percent of all Germans favored national self determination; see
http://ec.europa.eu/public_opinion/archives/eb/eb36/eb36_de.pdf, accessed 16 Apr. 2007.

[148] Lantis, *Strategic Dilemmas and the Evolution of German Foreign Policy since Unification*, 85.

[149] Lantis, *Strategic Dilemmas and the Evolution of German Foreign Policy since Unification*, 83.

[150] Libal, 78.

[151] Lantis, *Strategic Dilemmas and the Evolution of German Foreign Policy since Unification*, 86.

[152] Libal, 79.

German public opinion in the first months of the war was divided and moderate because the war had just started and attention was still focused on domestic issues surrounding reunification. A public research institute found out that while 34 percent of the public thought that recognition of the Yugoslav republics would endanger European policy, 39 percent thought that recognition was the only way to handle the crisis.[153]

The strong diversity of German political discourse highlights how the political parties found themselves caught between the peace rhetoric reflected in the "Berliner Programm" and the reality of the Balkan war. In retrospect, the war could not be settled without military force. Yet, the perception of the war was strongly influenced by domestic constraints. The culture of restraint predisposed the government to a diplomatic course of action. Political elites were constantly pressured by German society to take stronger action as the ethnic cleansing and the humanitarian tragedy unfolded. But the early German unilateralism of December 1991 was heavily criticized by other western governments.[154] Especially the Bush administration took umbrage to the perceived Germany pushiness over Slovenia and Croatia, which ran counter to a policy of Brent Scowcroft and Lawrence Eagleburger that sought to uphold the southern Slav status quo. Germany's nonconformist unilateral recognition attempt created a firestorm of criticism from international actors. Norms create political benefits for conformity and costs for nonconforming actions,[155] which is evidenced by the European reaction to Germany's efforts.

---

[153] Lantis, *Strategic Dilemmas and the Evolution of German Foreign Policy since Unification*, 85.

[154] The French government wanted to reject the German domination of the EC, within the context of the coming CFSP conference, so the recognition would be a multilateral act in an institutional framework rather than a spontaneous idea of the united Germany. The British government argued that the recognition, if any, should depend on a strict timeline, saying that recognition would worsen the Balkan situation because supporting one belligerent in an ethnic conflict antagonizes the other.

[155] Martha Finnemore, "Constructing Norms of Humanitarian Intervention," in *The Culture of National Security Norms and Identity in World Politics*, edited by Peter J. Katzenstein (New York: Columbia University Press, 1996), 183.

Adherence to multilateral norms, even knowing that it compromises effectiveness, is a testament to multilateralism.

2. Predispositions and Perceptions Caused by the International Environment

The main guideline for German foreign policy is the framework of rules and norms of International Organizations (IO). Due to its focus on multilateralism and integration, the Federal Republic is embedded in a close institutional web of IOs. On the one hand, Germany uses the framework of these organizations to pursue its national goals; on the other hand, institutional norms and rules restrict German foreign policy. Adenauer's Western orientated policy (Westpolitik) and Brandt's Eastern rapprochement policy (Ostpolitik) had lasting ramifications for German foreign policy and fostered its membership in various international organizations. The country followed a foreign policy of responsibility, even when the reunited Germany faced a fundamental reorientation of its foreign policy. Thus German predispositions towards the outbreak of the war have to be viewed through the lens of international organizations.

The dissolution of Yugoslavia was perceived from outside Europe as a European problem. More importantly, the European states, especially Germany and France, wanted to solve the crisis with a European effort. During a European Council meeting in late 1991, "western diplomats agreed that a fragmentation of the Yugoslavian federation would produce a complex mix of new challenges for economic and security relations in the region."[156] Thus, the European Community, including Germany and the U.S., fostered diplomatic negotiations to prevent dissolution of the Yugoslav state. Kohl and the parliament expected that EC diplomatic efforts to restore Yugoslavia would get strong domestic support. In fact, a research institute found out that 41 percent "trusted the European Community completely" to deal with the Balkan conflict, while 51 percent said they

---

[156] Lantis, *Strategic Dilemmas and the Evolution of German Foreign Policy since Unification*, 83.

trusted the EC to act appropriately.[157] However, the percentage of Germans who saw the EC initiatives as not useful and inappropriate rose steadily.[158] Public opinion pushed the German government to act. The unilateral decision to recognize Croatia and Slovenia caused fierce discussion in, and was not supported by, most EC members.[159] The Germans "faced an uphill battle and drew increasing criticism, even from their friends"[160] and Germany was viewed as a "saboteur within the European Community."[161] The Federal Republic was even blamed by the international community for prompting the war in Bosnia with its unilateral recognition attempt.[162] This accusation drove the German government into international passivity, even though its partners soon would adopt the German position on Milosevic and did not have any real alternative suggestion to keep the state together. In retrospect, the Bosnia verdict proved overdrawn.[163]

The major event at the start of 1991 was the military intervention of allied forces against Iraq after its August 1990 invasion of Kuwait. The invasion of Kuwait presented Germany with a serious

---

[157] Lantis, *Strategic Dilemmas and the Evolution of German Foreign Policy since Unification*, 85.

[158] Kommission der Europaeischen Gemeinschaft, *Eurobarometer: Die oeffentliche Meinung der Europaeischen Gemeinschaft, Nr. 36*, Generaldirektion Information, Kommunikation, Kultur. Umfragen, Forschung, Analysen (Bruessel: December 1991), http://ec.europa.eu/public_opinion/archives/eb/eb36/eb36_de.pdf, accessed 17 Apr.2007.

[159] Haftendorn, *Deutsche Aussenpolitik zwischen Selbstbeschraenkung und Selbstbehauptung 1945-2000*, 406.

[160] Lantis, *Strategic Dilemmas and the Evolution of German Foreign Policy since Unification*, 86. See also Gow, 171. Haftendorn, *Deutsche Aussenpolitik zwischen Selbstbeschraenkung und Selbstbehauptung 1945-2000*, 409.

[161] Libal, 75.

[162] American foreign minister Warren Christopher blamed the German government in *USA Today* for the Bosnian war; see *Süddeutsche Zeitung*, June, 1 1993.

[163] Gow, 171.

strategic dilemma in the midst of unification.[164] On the one hand, the German government, perceiving the Iraq occupation of Kuwait as a serious violation of international law, wanted to support the UN and the U.S. On the other hand, political elites were conscious of Soviet sensitivities and were cautious about hindering ongoing negotiations for German reunification and Soviet troop withdrawal. Germany's considerable financial and logistical support of Operation Desert Storm and the war in Iraq demonstrated its increased commitment to international security. However, deploying troops only to Turkey (not Kuwait), because this policy did not require amending the constitution, meant that Germany conformed to the culture of restraint, remained opposed to the use of force, and maintained negotiations with the Soviet Union.[165] Opinion polls found that 71 percent supported military action by the allies against Iraq.[166] After the Iraq war, trust in American political and military capabilities remained high.[167] The Iraqi rocket assault on Israel also worked to open the perspective of the more conservative figures in the German security elite as to the violent realities of what was soon to become a new era of turmoil.

The impact of the international environment, including multilateral obligations, rules and norms, is obvious. Germany was predisposed to act even more within the framework of international organizations after being blamed for its unilateral attempt to recognize Croatia and Slovenia. On the other hand, facing enormous domestic chal-

---

[164] By that time Germany was just in the final phase of the "two plus four treaty" negotiations concerning reunification. Further, the Federal Republic just negotiated about the withdrawal of all Soviet troops from the former GDR in the German-Soviet treaty; see Otte, *A Rising Middle Power? German Foreign Policy in Transformation*, 1989-1999, 91.

[165] Lantis, Strategic Dilemmas and the Evolution of German Foreign Policy since Unification, 47.

[166] 21 percent of Germans opposed the allied intervention. The enormous financial support of about DM 7 billion was backed by 57 percent of Germans. Even 56 percent favored the deployment of German troops to support Turkey in case the war sills over; see Lantis, *Strategic Dilemmas and the Evolution of German Foreign Policy since Unification*, 35.

[167] 73 percent of all Germans claimed their trust and confidence in the Americans; http://ec.europa.eu/public_opinion/archives/eb/eb35/eb35_en.pdf, accessed 17. Apr. 2007.

lenges from reunification and with its increased power, Germany had to act cautiously to avoid upsetting international actors.[168]

To summarize, German foreign policy was influenced by several external and internal factors just prior to the outbreak of the Bosnian war. Societal pressure, domestic political consensus, historical reverberations, multilateral conformity and compatibility, historical and economic ties, and the problems associated with reunification all influenced Germany's perceptions and approach to the Bosnian war.

C.   THE CHANGE IN GERMAN SECURITY CULTURE

This section guides the reader through the Bosnian war. It links aspects of the war, as the independent variable, with culture bearing units in Germany, representing the security culture; it analyzes public opinion and political discourse. This section is divided into three subsections. The first explains the transmittance of the Bosnian war to Germany and the importance of refugees and other means of communication. The following two subsections examine the change of security culture and its repercussions during the later years of the war. The last two subsections are chronologically structured to demonstrate the relatively rapid changes in the cultural bearing units.

In early 1994, two years before the Dayton agreement and three years after the outbreak of the war, the German political parties oriented their discourse and attitudes toward more effective involvement in and management of the Bosnian war, including the use of German military forces. This change was backed by steadily increasing public support for German political and military involvement. In the Bosnian war, Germany began to shed incrementally "some of its constitutional, if not political and psychological, inhibitions."[169] The acceptance of military involvement outside German territory and NATO commitments demonstrates a radical change in attitudes with-

---

[168] The Federal Republic government acknowledged to the Soviet Union that it would restrict its use of military forces in order to join an Atlantic alliance; see Haftendorn, *Deutsche Aussenpolitik zwischen Selbstbeschraenkung und Selbstbehauptung 1945-2000*, 387.

[169] Gow, 173.

in German society and political parties. The transformation culminated in Germany's military contributions to peace enforcement in the late Bosnian war, the Kosovo war and in Afghanistan.

1. The Role of Media and Refugees

The media became an important factor in the Bosnian war. They publicized political and military events with lasting repercussions for public opinion and policy. This was a three-year war, not counting the war in Slovenia and Croatia, with continuous, day-to-day coverage dominating the headlines. Specifically, news and images of Serb-built concentration camps as well as the siege of Sarajevo influenced attitudes, as did the bombing of Dubrovnik, the assault on Vukovar, the market place bombings in Sarajevo and the pictures of French blue helmets chained to Serb artillery as hostages.[170] Media influence is of course arguable. Its causal effect merges with many other stimuli that lead to changed behavior. Thus, it is said that the newspaper *Frankfurter Allgemeine Zeitung* was a catalyst for the government's early recognition attempt, a claim which major journalists of that paper in retrospect find doubtful.[171] But clearly, the media and the CNN effect as well as reporting from NGOs like Amnesty International made the public aware of human rights abuses.[172] The media was one reason that the Bosnian war was seen as occurring in the middle of Europe and thus requiring political action. After news coverage of attacks by demonstrators on Hans Koschnick, the former mayor of Bremen who was in 1994 EU Administrator for the divided city of Mostar, Koschnick was immediately recalled to Germany in a move similar to the later U.S. withdrawal from Somalia. Furthermore, the failure of the unarmed international police to safeguard Koschnick was a humil-

---

[170] Viktor Meier, "Die politische Bedeutung der Medien in der Konfliktbewaeltigung," in *Deutsche Konfliktbewaeltigung auf dem Balkan. Erfahrungen und Lehren aus dem Einsatz,* edited by Rafael Biermann (Baden-Baden: Nomos, 2002), 141.

[171] Meier, 141.

[172] Alan Dowty and Gil Loescher, "Refugee Flows as Grounds for International Action," in *Nationalism and Ethnic Conflict: Revised Edition,* edited by Michael E. Brown et al. (Cambridge, MA: MIT Press), 340.

iation for Western policy.[173] Germany, with its very high "media usage index," was especially affected by the media and press. Between 70 and 80 percent of Germans view the daily news on television.[174] The media as the transmitter of violence challenged public and elite beliefs.

The war in Bosnia-Herzegovina caused an exodus of about 1.5 million refugees.[175] The 350,000 refugees from the Balkan region who sought asylum in Germany were seen as a large scale refugee crisis. The refugees were human rights violations made visible.[176] Through eyewitness accounts and personal reports of atrocities, they transmitted the war directly into German households and to the parliament. Political elites could not afford to ignore the brutality and human rights abuses that uprooted entire ethnic groups once the conflict was internationalized with the "large-scale movement of people across national borders, under duress."[177] The indirect economic costs of refugee relief and assistance were an additional burden to the costs of reunification. The federal administration had to process over 120,000 applications for asylum alone from the former Yugoslavia in 1992.[178] The enormous amount of 350,000 refugees had to be billeted and accommodated for nearly three years in Germany. In fact the

---

[173] Meier, 145.

[174] Commission of the European Communities, *Eurobarometer: Public Opninion in the European Community, Nr. 37,* Directorate-General Information, Communication, Culture. Surveys, Research, Analyses (Brussels: Juni 1992), http://ec.europa.eu/public_opinion/archives/eb/eb37/eb37_en.pdf, 3/34, accessed 15 Apr. 2007. See also Commission of the European Communities, *Eurobarometer: Public Opninion in the European Community, Nr. 40,* Directorate-General Information, Communication, Culture. Surveys, Research, Analyses (Brussels: December 1993), http://ec.europa.eu/public_opinion/archives/eb/eb40/eb40_en.pdf, 49-51, accessed 15 Apr. 2007.

[175] Haftendorn, *Deutsche Aussenpolitik zwischen Selbstbeschraenkung und Selbstbehauptung 1945-2000,* 410.

[176] Dowty and Loescher, 364.

[177] Dowty and Loescher, 338.

[178] Rafael Biermann, *Lehrjahre im Kosovo: Das Scheitern der internationalen Krisenprävention vor Kriegsausbruch* (Paderborn: Ferdinand Schöningh, 2006), 615.

German administration financially supported households who were willing to accommodate and host refugees. But the normal procedure was that refugees were billeted in abandoned military barracks, camps, and housing boats. Those indirect costs associated with the accommodation and general assistance of refugees caused disorder and stressed the government. The humanitarian catastrophe, combined with disorder caused by refugees, produced a stronger mandate for governmental intervention.

2. The Impact of the Bosnian war

The German government did not anticipate the Bosnian war even though the wars in Croatia and Slovenia were clear examples of what might happen in this ethnically most mixed of the Yugoslav republics. Only three months after the outbreak of the war, the UN asked Germany to provide logistical support for UNPROFOR and advised of the possible need to deploy German troops. With the Bosnian war the German government immediately faced the need to go beyond diplomacy.[179] There was continual disagreement among the political parties on how to react to requests from the international community, with the strongest resistance from the SPD and the Greens. However, after clarifying the constitutional issues and with public support, the parties achieved a revised consensus on foreign policy.

a. *Early Restraints on Use of the Military*

In July 1992, the Security Council mandated the deployment of NATO and WEU warships to the Adriatic Sea to monitor the UN-imposed embargo on former Yugoslavia in Operation Sharp Guard. Manfred Woerner, the Secretary General of NATO, asked the German government to support the embargo with military units. Germany was also asked to deploy troops for UNPROFOR. There was strong domestic political division over supporting the embargo in the Adriatic Sea and UNPROFOR. The CDU strongly supported the par-

---

[179] Lantis, *Strategic Dilemmas and the Evolution of German Foreign Policy since Unification*, 88.

ticipation of German forces in the embargo and UNPROFOR.[180] Its coalition partner, the FDP, had strong concerns for historical reasons. The SPD argued that participation of German forces was unconstitutional and that the Basic Law had to be changed first. The SPD expert on foreign policy, Karsten Voigt, criticized the CDU, claiming that its support was "evidence of a larger government plan to expand the role of the Bundeswehr on a global scale."[181] Hans Ulrich Klose, the faction leader in parliament and shadow Defense Minister, threatened to challenge the case in the Constitutional Court, saying the SPD would "not permit a sneaking movement towards combat missions around the world."[182] Public opinion opposed military entanglement. The Allensbach public research institute found that only 12 percent of West Germans and 8 percent of East Germans supported contributing troops for UN peace enforcement, whereas 50 percent and 40 percent of West and East Germans, respectively, supported purely UN "blue helmet" missions.[183]

The German government decided to send naval forces for ground and air patrols to support the embargo in the Adriatic Sea. Public opinion was unsettled with this decision and the government

---

[180] The Chairman of the CDU/CSU Foreign Affairs Committee of the Bundestag, Karl-Heinz Hornhues offered public support for the deployment of German troops to the region and pledged military support of future peacekeeping missions. The deputy chairman of the CDU/CSU Fraktion even supported precision strikes against Serb airports and missile bases with the participation of German troops; see Lantis, *Strategic Dilemmas and the Evolution of German Foreign Policy since Unification*, 89.

[181] Lantis, *Strategic Dilemmas and the Evolution of German Foreign Policy since Unification*, 90.

[182] Lantis, *Strategic Dilemmas and the Evolution of German Foreign Policy since Unification*, 91.

[183] Research found that 28 percent of West Germans and 42 percent of East Germans opposed any participation with UN forces; see Elisabeth Noelle-Neumann and Renate Köcher, eds., *Allensbacher Jahrbuch der Demoskopie* (München: K. G. Saur, 1993), 1095.

lost part of its electorate.[184] CDU and FDP argued that contributing to international efforts was a political necessity. The FDP's historical concerns were countered by the Foreign Minister Klaus Kinkel's claim that Germany should no longer behave like an "impotent dwarf."[185] However, support to UNPROFOR was denied. The German government "made clear that German forces were only to monitor commercial traffic" within the embargo and that they had to remain at least 15 nautical miles off the Balkan coastline in international waters.[186] Kohl's strategy toward this and other small scale deployments was, first, to let them be challenged in court to affirm their constitutionality; second, to implicitly change the interpretation of the Basic Law; third, to open the window for a gradual increase in troop deployments; and fourth, to change public opinion by dedicated but careful leadership.[187]

b.   Self Reflection

The humanitarian situation in Bosnia continued to deteriorate in the winter of 1992. The media showed war atrocities more frequently and an increasing number of refugees sought asylum in Germany. Information filtering out of Bosnia reveled that Bosnian-Serb forces practice "ethnic cleansing" and refuse to abide to the Geneva Convention, how to treat prisoner of war. International pressure on the Kohl administration became stronger and public opinion changed with more images of the atrocities. Researchers found meanwhile that 62 percent of Germans believed that the government should take a more asser-

---

[184] In August 1992, Allensbach found that 54 percent of West Germans and 36 percent of East Germans agreed to the naval support of the embargo; see Noelle-Neumann and Köcher, eds., *Allensbacher Jahrbuch der Demoskopie*, 1095. An EMNID public opinion research project figured out that in elections after the deployment decision, the CDU would have lost 8 percent of their voters and the SPD would have won 6 percent; see Lantis, *Strategic Dilemmas and the Evolution of German Foreign Policy since Unification*, 88-92.

[185] Duffield, 195.

[186] Lantis, *Strategic Dilemmas and the Evolution of German Foreign Policy since Unification*, 91.

[187] Johnston, 272.

tive role in international affairs and 53 percent believed that the German military should participate in peacekeeping operations without restraint.[188] The agreement to participate in UN blue helmet missions rose accordingly to 67 percent in West Germany and 55 percent in East Germany.[189] In December 1992, 81 percent said that Germany should work towards a common defense policy, while 75 percent were for a common foreign policy of the EC.[190]

In response to public attitudes, the German government began to reflect on the efficacy of a policy that increasingly seemed betwixt and between of an international environment devoid of perpetual peace. In a speech in September 1993, the Foreign Minister said that Germany should not criticize other actors trying to end the crisis in the Balkans while it does not want to carry a "heavier burden of responsibility in the region."[191] He himself was the politician in Germany most exposed to growing pressure from international partners to contribute more significantly to the peace effort in Bosnia. The SPD thought that its strict aversion to German forces in the Bosnian war was in the long term untenable. The parliamentary leader Hans Ulrich Klose claimed that the highly restrictive position of the SPD would make them "look ridiculous."[192] The opposition partner Green Party was stuck in a moral dilemma. On the one hand, the Greens represented the pacifist electorate in Germany and saw the pursuit of peace as among its most important goals. On the other hand, the pro-

---

[188] Lantis, *Strategic Dilemmas and the Evolution of German Foreign Policy since Unification*, 96.

[189] By April 1993, agreement with German participation in the UN peace enforcing mission rose to 39 percent in the West and 23 percent in the East; see Noelle-Neumann and Köcher, eds., *Allensbacher Jahrbuch der Demoskopie*, (München: K.G.Saur, 1997), 1147.

[190] Commission of the European Communities, *Eurobarometer: Public Opninion in the European Community, Nr. 38,* Directorate-General Information, Communication, Culture. Surveys, Research, Analyses (Brussels: December 1992), http://ec.europa.eu/public_opinion/archives/eb/eb38/eb38_en.pdf, accessed 17 April 2007.

[191] Lantis, *Strategic Dilemmas and the Evolution of German Foreign Policy since Unification*, 98.

[192] Duffield, 202.

longed war and violence in the Balkans showed the party that diplomatic efforts alone were not sufficient to stop the Bosnian war.

With Resolution 781, the UN Security Council decided on a no-fly zone over Bosnia in October 9, 1992. The zone had to be controlled by NATO AWACS aircraft. Ironically, not only were they stationed in Geilenkirchen, Germany, but almost a third of the early warning aircraft crews were German. The withdrawal of the German aircrews would have sacrificed their operational capability and thus the mission. It would have also dealt a serious blow to NATO cohesion and German responsibility in the Alliance. The AWACS crisis was another landmark in transforming German security culture. The CDU and FDP coalition faced its strongest challenge when the CDU unilaterally tried to amend the Basic Law to allow the use of military force. Foreign Minister Kinkel threatened in January 1993 that, due to the constitutional situation, the FDP would withdraw German aircrews from the AWACS mission, while CSU Chairman Theo Waigel called the FDP whiners.[193] Yet the FDP successfully pressured its coalition partners CDU and CSU to accept a compromise and to amend the constitutional Basic Law. The amendment of Article 24 in the Basic Law was intended to bridge the gap between Article 24 and Article 87a. The amendment dealt with the deployment of German forces to UN peacekeeping missions, requiring that deployments receive majority support from the Bundestag. With the internal government compromise, the FDP finally agreed to the AWACS participation. However, the SPD said the amendment would be "dead on arrival" and the Green party opposed to the AWACS deployment.[194] The SPD politicians warned the cabinet that the move was a step toward gunboat diplomacy ("einem Rückfall zur Denkweise der Kanonenbootdiplomatie des Wilhelminismus").[195] The SPD implied that

---

193 Lantis, *Strategic Dilemmas and the Evolution of German Foreign Policy since Unification*, 96.

194 Lantis, *Strategic Dilemmas and the Evolution of German Foreign Policy since Unification*, 96.

195 Lantis, *Strategic Dilemmas and the Evolution of German Foreign Policy since Unification*, 96. The SPD compared the policy of the coalition with German imperialism in Prussia under Wilhelm the Great. Prussia sent heavily armed boats along coastlines and rivers to control and safeguard its colonies.

German participation in AWACS aircraft had nothing to do with humanitarian intervention and was therefore unconstitutional. However, in 1993, the Constitutional Court decided in favor of German aircrew participating in the AWACS operation "Deny Flight." The court based its decision on the fact that AWACS aircraft would not have operational capability without the German aircrews. Withdrawing German troops would seriously harm the success of the operation.

c. The Political Change

With Germany's EC presidency in late 1993 and the establishment of the Contact Group in February 1994, Germany reentered the international scene. After the bombing raid on Sarajevo in the same month created "a firestorm of controversy in about how to respond,"[196] German domestic attitudes changed dramatically. Public opinion held that the Bosnian Serb aggression was comparable with everything banned in Germany after the Second World War: communism, nationalism and militarism and the repression of small states.

Germany was asked unofficially to participate in air strikes with combat forces, specifically Tornado bombers for reconnaissance and suppression of enemy air defense. The Constitutional Court decided that German participation in UN-authorized international military operations outside NATO territory did not violate the constitution.[197] This historical ruling ended the internal government debate about the constitutionality of using military force which had begun with the AWACS crisis in early 1993. The objective of the federal Constitutional Court's ruling was to establish a definite judgment on the issue of German out-of-area troop deployments and the political requirements for such actions.[198] While CDU/CSU and their coalition partner FDP argued that Germany must be involved with the

---

[196] Lantis, *Strategic Dilemmas and the Evolution of German Foreign Policy since Unification*, 99.

[197] The German Basic Law poses no obstacle to deploy German forces, providing that the Bundestag gives specific constitutional approval for such a deployment. See Nolte, 234.

[198] Lantis, *Strategic Dilemmas and the Evolution of German Foreign Policy since Unification*, 108.

UN operation to secure world peace, SPD and the Green Party continued to argue that the Basic Law prohibited out-of-area operations, which were seen as a dangerous foreign policy expansion.[199] In July 12, 1994, the Constitutional Court decided that the deployment of the Bundeswehr was permissible under Article 24 of the Basic Law. This decision closed the chapter on jurisdictional struggle and put German foreign policy on a new path.[200] On December 2, 1994 the SPD leader Rudolf Scharping stated his opposition to using German Tornado jets over Bosnian territory, and foreign affairs expert Guenther Verheugen declared that NATO involvement in the conflict would increase atrocities, saying the SPD should refuse any deployment of German ground troops.[201]

However, after the official NATO request to protect the UNPROFOR withdrawal with German military forces, the SPD political disposition changed to favor the deployment of forces for humanitarian purposes. Mirroring a traditional schism in the ranks of the German Social Democrats, some SPD politicians voiced full support for the NATO request.[202] One week later, Scharping declared that his party would not oppose the German Tornado operations in support

---

[199] Kinkel argued that the UN was becoming "the central guardian of peace for the human race … Germany has to come down from the spectator's gallery." See Lantis, *Strategic Dilemmas and the Evolution of German Foreign Policy since Unification,* 109.

[200] Following the Constitutional Court ruling, Foreign Minister Kinkel argued that the aim was not to militarize the German foreign policy, but to establish a situation in which Germany, like every other country, could freely decide whether to use its armed forces in each individual case. Defense Minister Volker Ruehe claimed that because the Bundeswehr is prepared for the unlikely need for territorial defense and treaty obligations, but not for the likely need for international crisis management, the Bundeswehr needs fundamental reform. See Lantis, *Strategic Dilemmas and the Evolution of German Foreign Policy since Unification,* 111.

[201] "Entscheidung ueber Tornadoeinsatz naechste Woche," *German News*, Deutsche Ausgabe, 02.12.1994, http://www.germnews.de/gn/1994/12/02, and "Bundesregierung verschiebt Entscheidung ueber Kampfflugzeug-Einsatz," *German News*, Deutsche Ausgabe, 07.12.1994, http://www.germnews.de/gn/1994/12/07, accessed 19 Mar.2007.

[202] "Bundeswehr soll vielleicht bei UN-Truppenrueckzug Hilfe leisten," *German News*, Deutsche Ausgabe, 13.12.1994, http://www.germnews.de/gn/1994/12/13, accessed 19 Mar 2007.

of an eventual UNPROFOR retreat and humanitarian relief convoys. This decision caused a rift in the SPD. The deputy party leader Wieczorek-Zeul argued that Scharping would willingly lead the SPD and Germany into war.[203] To settle the dispute within his party, Scharping declared that the SPD did not decide in favor of NATO support, but that humanitarian relief must be considered. The issue required negotiation in the Bundestag, but two days before Christmas the government and the SPD opposition declared their full support for the NATO request, a decision with broad public support.[204]

The political parties displayed unity in the wake of the NATO request to support the UN withdrawal. Scharping condemned the Serb attacks and declared his agreement with government efforts to intervene more effectively.[205] He also said that the SPD would support deploying military aircraft to protect UN relief flights.[206] Even Klose characterized support for the air strikes as correct. Scharping was able to overcome disputes within the SPD with his emphasis on humanitarian aid and his tactical decision to withhold his final decision until just before Christmas, which increased his public support. Public opinion research found that 75 percent of Germans supported the use of military force for humanitarian purposes. This marked the greatest change in German policy and public attitudes during the war.

---

[203] "Aeusserungen zu den geplanten Tornado-Einsaetzen," *German News*, Deutsche Ausgabe, 18.12.1994, http://www.germnews.de/gn/1994/12/18, accessed 19 Mar 2007.

[204] "Regierung und SPD im Grundsatz ueber Bundeswehr-Einsatz einig," *German News*, Deutsche Ausgabe, 22.12.1994, http://www.germnews.de/gn/1994/12/22, accessed 19 Mar 2007. Over 25.000 people demonstrated in Bonn for peace in Bosnia; see Lantis, *Strategic Dilemmas and the Evolution of German Foreign Policy since Unification,* 99.

[205] The SPD claimed that they have no serious differences on foreign policy with the CDU. All policy leaders basically voiced support for participation in air strikes and characterized those as justified, necessary and right.

[206] "Interview mit Außenminister Klaus Kinkel (FDP)," *Bild am Sonntag,* 19 December 1994.

The Repercussions of Change

In 1995, the Bosnian war took on an added dimension. Pictures of the July 1995 Srebrenica massacre were spread all over Europe. Croatia's offensive against the Serb Army changed the power distribution in the Balkans. In May 1995, about 300 UN peacekeepers were taken as hostages. The Bosnian Serbs threatened to use them as human shields if the NATO air strikes persisted. The July 6 Serb artillery attack on Srebrenica caused the final change in German peacekeeping efforts in Bosnia. The European governments and the North Atlantic Council members declared the actions of the Bosnian Serbs unacceptable and threatened that NATO forces would respond with the use of force. They "began to consider the deployment of ground troops to galvanize a diplomatic, political, economic, and military endgame in the conflict."[207] Those ground troops would consist of a Rapid Reaction Force (RRF) to safeguard UNPROFOR.

Germany was asked to deploy German forces to the RRF. In addition to widespread public agreement on German responsibility in the Balkan crisis, there was a growing political consensus for military action. Polls showed that Germans strongly supported active contribution to NATO missions. Between unification and 1995, public support for the alliance had increased steadily. Public support for NATO was 57 percent in 1991, but by 1995 it had increased to 71 percent. One survey institute found that 74 percent of all respondents indicated that they would support NATO involvement in a new crisis on Europe's periphery.[208] The most significant change occurred within the political elites of the Green Party. Joschka Fischer, a member of the Green Party's board of directors and later Foreign Minister in the SPD/Green Coalition, called for a redefinition of his strongly

---

[207] Lantis, *Strategic Dilemmas and the Evolution of German Foreign Policy since Unification,* 116.

[208] Lantis, *Strategic Dilemmas and the Evolution of German Foreign Policy since Unification,* 99 and 121.

pacifist party's principles on foreign policy.[209] During a conference on peacekeeping operations and German responsibilities in fall 1995, the Green Party for the first time considered how and when to deploy the German military for peace operations.[210] In a historic speech, Fischer revoked the pacifist phrase "nie wieder Krieg," never again war, changing it to "nie wieder Auschwitz," never again Auschwitz. He thus introduced the need for military force in Green foreign policy.[211] He contended that the party should support German contributions to peacekeeping blue-helmet missions to stop the atrocities in Bosnia while holding firm to nonviolence.[212] His speech set Green Party politics on a new course and was path breaking for all of German foreign policy.

An editorial in the Berlin newspaper *Tagesspiegel* summed up the atmosphere, saying "the government's decision has been made and it holds no surprises. Germany will participate in protecting the UN Blue Helmets in the former Yugoslavia. Although it sounds like a routine decision, in reality it marks the close of a chapter of German

---

[209] In a letter to leading party members, Fischer addressed the dilemma of party negation of military force and the use of military means to stop the atrocities in Bosnia. See Steffen Schmuck-Soldan, *Der Pazifismus bei Buendnis 90/ Die Gruenen: Entwicklung und Stellenwert einer aussenpolitischen Ideologie 1990-2000*, chapter 9.2., http://edoc.hu-berlin.de/dissertationen/schmuck-soldan-steffen-2004-05-03/HTML/front.html, accessed 23 May 2007.

[210] In a compromise in early 1995, the Green Party opposed any German military contribution to the RRF, but strongly supported increasing German support of humanitarian relief operations. See Schmuck-Soldan, chapter 9.1; Lantis, *Strategic Dilemmas and the Evolution of German Foreign Policy since Unification*, 128.

[211] "Nie wieder Krieg" was the deeply rooted historical notion of German society, especially in the pacifist electorate after World War II. Fischer used the phrase "nie wieder Auschwitz" to remind not only his party of the atrocities of Nazi Germany and as an indirect comparison with the violence of the Bosnian war. The rhetorical preference of "nie wieder Krieg" was incompatible with coherent foreign policy during the Bosnian war. Fischer stressed the real political consequences of pacifism to the Green Party and emphasized Germany's moral obligations in international politics. See also Rudolf Burger, "Nationale Ethik: Illusion und Realitaet," in *Hamburger Ausblicke* 2 (2006), 83, http://archiv.hausrissen.org/pdf/ausblicke/2-2006/Burger%20-%20Nationale%20Interessen.pdf, accessed 23 May 2007.

[212] Lantis, *Strategic Dilemmas and the Evolution of German Foreign Policy since Unification*, 128.

security policy."[213] Closing the chapter on the culture of restraint, Germany deployed 1,500 German troops to Croatia and built logistical support and a field hospital to support the Implementation Force (IFOR). The decision to contribute German forces to IFOR passed the Bundestag by an overwhelming 543 to 107 votes with strong public support.[214] The German contribution to IFOR, though still outside of Bosnia, consisted of heavy armored combat troops and special forces.

D.   CONCLUSION

Comparing German security and defense policy before and after the Bosnian war, a drastic change is evident. The policy of restraint gave way to a policy more focused on Germany's international responsibility, institutionally harnessed and multilaterally legitimized in the midst of an international system in flux and the return of war to Europe and its environs. Skepticism in German political culture about the use of German forces was reduced significantly, eclipsed by humanitarian concerns that were eventually accepted by the German left as well. The public bias against military entanglement was challenged by eyewitness accounts of refugees from ethnic cleansing, and the CNN effect brought images of war atrocities into German households well familiar with the locales and human faces of such violence. Faced with 350,000 refugees, domestic German policy noted that the "creation of refugees is most indisputably a creation of 'international disorder.'"[215] The world media reports of the Bosnian catastrophe and the "combination of humanitarian concerns and the impact of disorder" interacted synergistically to produce broad acceptance of intervention and the use of military force.[216] The media and refugees challenged images of a peaceful Europe and German pacifist ideas.

---

[213] Lantis, *Strategic Dilemmas and the Evolution of German Foreign Policy since Unification*, 122.

[214] Lantis, *Strategic Dilemmas and the Evolution of German Foreign Policy since Unification*, 130.

[215] Dowty and Loescher, 364.

[216] Dowty and Loescher, 364.

The guiding principles and behavior of German foreign policy are based on both external and internal dimensions. The examination of foreign policy requires linking the internal predispositions, such as values, norms, and culture, with the international environment. In other words, foreign policy change depends strongly upon compatibility and consensus. Compatibility accounts for "the degrees of feasibility of various foreign policy goals," in light of the international environment.[217] Consensus is "the amount of domestic political agreement regarding the ends and means of foreign policy change."[218] The internal predispositions of Germany's public and political elites determined both the compatibility of their views with the international context and the consensus needed to act.

The interests, values and norms that guided German foreign policy changed because they were incompatible with the international environment and were not backed by public consensus. Faced with the Bosnian war, the subjective and often unquestioned assumptions about the political world that had guided German foreign policy for decades were transformed in an agonizing process to fit the new international environment.

---

[217] Wolfram Hanrieder, "Compatibility and Consensus: A Proposal for the Conceptual Linkage of External and Internal Dimensions of Foreign Policy," *American Political Science Review* 61, no.4 (Dec. 1967), 1977.

[218] Lantis, *Strategic Dilemmas and the Evolution of German Foreign Policy since Unification*, 7.

V.   UNITED STATES SECURITY CULTURE

A.   U.S. HISTORY, FOREIGN AND MILITARY POLICY DISPOSITIONS

This section examines the sources and development of the security culture of the United States of America, emphasizing the rationale for U.S. cultural preferences and explaining the cultural predispositions of the American public and political elites. The chapter will, despite the preceding chapter on German security culture, put more emphasize on the examination of military culture, since security and military culture are more closely related in the U.S. than in Germany and influence each other.

Both history and geography shape the national security culture of the United States.[219] Isolated with relatively weak neighbors on the American continent, shielded by the Atlantic and Pacific oceans from the Eurasian landmass, the U.S. has a form of free security. This security free ride insulated America from the destruction of the European wars. Nor did the U.S. exhaust itself by waging wars against its neighbors like the European powers. Long periods of peace on its own ter-

---

[219] On the U.S. strategic history, security culture and military culture, this author relied on following works: Bernard Brodie, *Strategy in the Missile Age* (Princeton: Princeton University Press, 1959); Colin Dueck, *Reluctant Crusaders: Power, Culture, and Change in American Grand Strategy* (Princeton: Princeton University Press, 2006); Colin S. Gray, *Modern Strategy* (Oxford: Oxford University Press, 1999); Colin S. Gray, "Strategy in the Nuclear Age: The United States, 1945-1991" in *The Making of Strategy* edited by Williamson Murray, MacGregor Knox, and Alvin H. Bernstein (New York: Cambridge University Press, 1994); George F. Kennan, *American Diplomacy: Expanded Edition* (Chicago: University of Chicago Press, 1984); Michael Lind, *The American Way of Strategy* (New York: Oxford University Press, 2006); Allan R. Millett et al., *For the Common Defense: A Military History of the United States of America* (New York: Free Press, 1984); Walter Millis, ed., *American Military Thought* (New York: Bobbs-Merrill, 1966); Peter Paret, et al., eds., *Makers of Modern Strategy: From Machiavelli to the Nuclear Age* (Princeton: Princeton University Press, 1986); Richard J. Payne, *The Clash with Distant Cultures: Values, Interests, and Force in American Foreign Policy* (Albany: State University of New York Press, 1995); Emory Upton, *The Military Policy of the United States* (New York: Greenwood, 1968); Russell F. Weigley, *The American Way of War: A History of United States Military Strategy and Policy* (Bloomington: Indiana University Press, 1973).

ritory punctuated by conflicts like the civil war and the two world wars shaped America's national security culture. Those conflicts are seen as crusades of good versus evil.[220] American security culture rejected the European tradition of power politics based on the dynastic absolutist model and the power-balancing alliance politics of Bismarck.[221] Americans "felt both separate from—indeed, superior to—a Europe perceived as corrupt, effete, maybe downright degenerate."[222] Moreover, wars were fought outside American territory with relative ease,[223] specifically when compared with European powers.

The free security realm affects American perception of the world and other states.[224] The U.S. does not perceive itself as a nation among others "with whom it must deal as rivals, as allies, as partners."[225] Imitating their British progenitors, Americans for a long time identified themselves as an exceptional society with a particular

[220] Samuel P. Huntington, *The Soldier and the State: The Theory and Practice of Civil-Military Relations* (Cambridge, MA: Belknap Press, 1957), 152.

[221] President Woodrow Wilson went to war not to preserve the balance of power but to destroy it; see John Lamberton Harper, *American Visions of Europe* (Cambridge: University Press, 1996), 30. Morgenthau argues that the aversion to power politics is rooted in the isolation of the American continent during the nineteenth century and the humanitarian pacifism and anti-imperialism of American ideology; see Hans J. Morgenthau, *Politics Among Nations* (Chicago: University of Chicago Press, 1948), 19.

[222] Justus D. Doeneke, *Storm on the Horizon: The Challenge to American Intervention, 1939-1941* (Lanham: Rowman and Littlefield Publishers, 2003), xi.

[223] Combined with the devastating destructions in Europe, the Americans have lost fewer than 425,000 lives during the second world war, whereas the Russians lost about 20 million; see Thomas Walker, "American Uniqueness, Strategic Culture and the Origins of the Transatlantic Rift," paper presented at the International Studies Association meetings, Chicago, March 2007, 5.

[224] Anxieties about security have kept the growth of optimism within bounds among other peoples. The relative absence of such anxieties, along with other factors, helped to make optimism a national philosophy in the U.S.; see C. Vann Woodward, "The Age of Reinterpretation," *American Historical Review 66* (Oct. 1960), 6; Walker, 4.

[225] Walter Lippmann, *Public Opinion and Foreign Policy in the United States* (London: Allen and Unwin, 1952), 25-26.

obligation to better the lot of humanity.[226] The U.S. understood aggression like the European wars as rebellion against the eternal and universal principles of world society. Therefore the dominant impulse of U.S. foreign policy was to diffuse its liberal democratic ideals, linking closely democracy and peace. American idealism, associated with the "American way of life," is a core-element of its national identity that considers the U.S. as a model for others. Idealism proposes that all countries should live together in peace, justice and wealth. This so-called one world concept based on a liberal democratic world order was advocated by the U.S. throughout its history.[227] Creating a world order and secure international environment to enhance the nation's economic well-being and promote U.S. goods abroad is in America's national interest.[228] Thus, idealism, and specifically the promotion of American values and the free market system abroad, happily coincides with America's national interests.

---

[226] W. H. Brands, *What America Owes the World* (Cambridge: Cambridge University Press, 2000), vii.

[227] Wilson was a fervent advocate of American idealism. He stressed the transfer of liberal democracy and economic interference for European reconstruction in the post-world war era. He developed a fourteen-point program based on Kant's theory of a Pacific Union. On the Pacific Union, see Bruce M. Russet et al., *Grasping the Democratic Peace Principles for a Post Cold War World* (Princeton: Princeton University Press, 1993), 4. For detailed information on Wilson, see Arthur S. Link, *Woodrow Wilson: Revolution, War, and Peace* (Arlington Heights, Ill.: AHM Publisher Corp., 1979). Two schools of thought identify how the U.S. promotes a more liberal world order. The "crusaders" argue that the U.S. must promote democracy and freedom abroad, by force if necessary. The "exemplarists" argue that the U.S. best advertises liberal ideals abroad by example; see Dueck, 23.

[228] The purpose of the American way of strategy is to defend the American way of life, preferably by means that do not endanger the American way of life; see Lind, *The American Way of Strategy*, 252. On U.S. national interests see Donald E. Nuechterlein, *America Recommitted: A Superpower Assesses Its Role in a Turbulent World*, *2nd Edition* (Lexington: University Press of Kentucky, 2001), 15-17.

But American idealism has its limits and critics.[229] With its unique willingness to engage in warfare, the U.S. tends to rely on and emphasize the efficacy of military force, often as some scholars controversially argue, without a majority of the public agreeing.[230] As with the two world wars, Americans prefer wars with definitive results.[231] Since 1945, U.S. military leaders have been uncomfortable with the conduct of war for limited political aims. In Korea and Vietnam, the military leadership did not like anything short of total victory.[232] *The American Way of War* by Weigley describes the distinct American military culture that favors wars of annihilation through the

---

[229] George F. Kennan argues that U.S. international relations were characterized by excessive moralism and legalism that might lead to crusades against the perceived evil. A war fought in the name of high moral principle finds no end short of total domination; see George F. Kennan, *American Diplomacy*, expanded edition (Chicago: University of Chicago Press, 1984), 100. Samuel P. Huntington argues that Americans tend to be extremists on the subject of war: they either embrace war wholeheartedly or reject it completely. Since liberalism deprecates the moral validity of the interests of the state in security, war must be either condemned as incompatible with liberal goals or justified as an ideological movement in support of those goals; see Huntington, 151.

[230] Robert Kagan, *Of Paradise and Power: America and Europe in the New World Order* (New York: Vintage, 2003) 106. On the question of consensus, imperial elites tend to rely less on domestic support to produce military power. The costs of war might be borne or shared with colonies and allies; see Theo Farrel, "Strategic Culture and American Empire," *SAIS Review* 25.2 (2005), 5. Scholars often refer to the American empire as the dominant narrative of the 21st century; see Joseph S. Nye, Jr., "American Power and Strategy after Iraq," *Foreign Affairs* 82, no. 4 (2003), 60. The U.S. might not see itself as an empire, but its behavior is perceived as imperial by other states; see Dimitri K. Simes, "America's Imperial Dilemma," *Foreign Affairs* 82, no. 6 (2003), 93.

[231] The reason to fight wars that produce partial victory and compromise with evil is that wars generally become moral crusades. This explains the tension between the idealist dislike of violence and their use of force. See Payne, 47-54. Decisive warfare became something of a sacred writ of American strategic doctrine; see Donald Abenheim, *Soldiers and Politics Transformed: German-American Reflections on Civil-Military Relations in a New Strategic Environment* (Berlin: Carole Hartmann Miles-Verlag, 2006), 58. The influence of Jomini on American strategic doctrine is also notable; see Baron de Jomini, *The Art of War* (Westport: Greenwood Press), 16-19, 65-198.

[232] See "The Testimony of General Douglas MacArthur" in Allen Guttmann, ed., *Korea: Cold War and Limited War*, 2nd ed. (New York: D. C. Heath, 1972).

extensive use of firepower.[233] Other ways of conducting war have been manifested in American military culture, including deterrence and wars for limited aims.[234] Overall, however, the American way of fighting wars is the "quest for swift victory through the hazards of decisive battle rather than [a] slower approach."[235] Americans seem to prefer "neat categories of right and wrong, and clear indications of national interest;" and they dislike limited liability.[236]

To achieve fast and decisive victories, U.S. military strategy relies strongly on technology. The apocalyptical warfare during the air war against Japan was made possible by military leaders and technicians' "technological fanaticism."[237] Throughout the Cold War, the United States sought to use its qualitative advantage to counterbalance the numerical conventional superiority of the Soviet Union. President John F. Kennedy announced the doctrine of "flexible response," a concept of controlled use of force appropriate to specific conditions. Response to attacks would be "'suitable, selective' as well as 'swift and effective.'"[238] The Strategic Defense Initiative (SDI) under the Reagan Administration is an example of techno-centric warfare. Conversely, the nuclear arsenal of the U.S. creates the notion of a sharp dichotomy between war and peace. Throughout the Cold War, nuclear weapons have been predominantly perceived as a means

---

[233] Weigley, *The American Way of War: A History of United States Military Strategy and Policy.*

[234] Brian M. Linn, "*The American Way of War* Revisited," *Journal of Military History* 66 no. 2 (April 2002), 501-533.

[235] Gray, "Strategy in the Nuclear Age: The United States, 1945-1991," 594-595.

[236] The Balkan conflict did not present itself as a clear choice between good and evil. Future conflicts will more likely require choosing the lesser of two evils, with U.S. interests ambiguous and no vital interest directly threatened; see Robert A. Vitas and John Allen Williams, eds., "Nagging Conflicts," in *U.S. National Security Policy and Strategy 1987-1994: Documents and Policy Proposals* (Westport: Greenwood Press, 1996), 245. Limited liability can be defined as a culturally shaped preference for avoiding costs and commitments in grand strategy to an extent that is actually inconsistent with stated and established international goals; see Dueck, 26.

[237] Michael Sherry quoted in Farrel, "Strategic Culture and American Empire," 8.

[238] Gordon A. Craig and Alexander L. George, *Force and Statecraft: Diplomatic Problems of Our Time,* 3rd ed. (New York: Oxford University Press, 1995), 260.

of deterrence in Europe and to a lesser extent as means of limited nuclear war fighting for the U.S. Nevertheless, the destructiveness of
nuclear weapons makes them unsuitable "as an instrument for the
achievement of any coherent political purpose."[239] Nuclear weapons
are perceived as politically, militarily, and psychologically different;
their use is perceived as taboo.[240]

With the collapse of the Soviet Union, the prospect of nuclear
war faded. As the only remaining superpower, and with the worldwide reduction of military budgets, America's technological advantage
increased. Post-Cold War conflicts like the war in the former Yugoslavia highlighted the technological rift. But U.S. military technological superiority can be both functional and dysfunctional.[241] With the
advent of the new world order, the U.S. embraced the "new American way of war" or the so called revolution in military affairs based on
extremely low cost, low risk military intervention.[242] Washington was
able to "pick and choose" among conflicts and crises according to its
interest.[243]

America's traditional reliance on military technology was not
always a means for success. Despite large scale industrialized air offensives against North Vietnam, that war did not end with American

---

[239] George F. Kennan quoted in Chris Hables Gray, *Postmodern War: The New Politics of Conflict* (London: Routledge, 1997), 138.

[240] Nina Tannenwald, "Stigmatizing the Bomb: Origins of the Nuclear Taboo,"
International Security 29, no. 4 (Spring 2005), 5. When Secretary of State John Foster
Dulles in January 1954 announced that "massive retaliation" would be the admin-
istration policy, he implied that the U.S. would respond to low-level aggression
against its allies with strategic nuclear attacks, alarming Americans and the Allies.
This led Dulles to clarify and moderate his meaning; see Craig and George, 259.

[241] The machine-mindedness so prominent in the American way of war is inher-
ently neither functional nor dysfunctional. When it inclines Americans to seek what
amounts to a technological rather than a political peace, and when it dictates tactics
regardless of political context, then it is dysfunctional. However, prudent and inno-
vative exploitation of the technological dimensions of strategy and war can be a
vital asset; see Gray, *Modern Strategy*, 147.

[242] The new way of war involved airstrikes, cruise missiles, precision guided weapons, arms sales and the reliance on proxy forces; see Dueck, 140.

[243] Susan Woodward, *Balkan Tragedy: Chaos and Dissolution after the Cold War* (Washington D.C.: Brookings Institution, 1995), 397.

victory even though the U.S. did not lose a single battle in the Vietnam campaign and its technological power remained potent throughout the war.[244] The declared strategy in Vietnam failed to bring success, especially in counter insurgency. The issue duration caused by the new strategy, including losses of U.S. soldiers, turned the public against the war. By 1967, President Lyndon B. Johnson and Secretary of Defense Robert McNamara knew the war could not be won. The military, and specifically General MacArthur, felt that the war was lost by a "stab in the back."[245] In fact, Vietnam was perceived as a debacle for the U.S. It had lasting ramifications on the American way of war—causing the "Vietnam syndrome." As an outgrowth of the collective lesson of Vietnam and subsequent conflicts, the Weinberger doctrine promulgated a list of conditions for the U.S. commitment of troops.[246]

Modern day casualty aversion in U.S. security culture, partly caused by the Vietnam debacle, is deeply rooted in the public and elite's psyche. The coffins of American soldiers, amid the strategic pointlessness of Johnson and Nixon's strategies, "eroded U.S. domestic support for the war in the mid- to late-1960s."[247] Military leaders and politicians, more than the public, feel the sensitivity to casualties in war. The responsibility elites feel for the public weigh heavily when

---

[244] Another pillar of U.S. military strategy is the tendency to industrialize war. Prolonged humanitarian aid flights in Bosnia, training Croat forces and arms sales, and the extensive NATO bombardment of Serb strongholds accounted for the industrialization of war.

[245] The stab in the back is a pattern of argumentation that comes up when civilians refuse to support their soldiers because of perceived timid leadership or home front mopery; see Abenheim, 147.

[246] According the Weinberger doctrine the U.S. should not commit forces to combat unless a vital national interest of the U.S. or its allies are involved. Those troops should only be committed wholeheartedly and with a clear intention of winning. Political and military objectives should be defined clearly and be possible to accomplish. The relationship among objectives and the size and composition of forces should be continually reassessed and adjusted if necessary. A reasonable assurance of public and Congressional support must be secured prior committing forces to battle. Finally, the commitment of forces should always be the last resort.

[247] Farrel, "Strategic Culture and American Empire," 8.

they send the army of the American people into war.[248] Junior officers and the public "appear to be more prepared to accept risk, provided the mission serves some purpose."[249] The political fallout of the Vietnam conflict left its mark on all subsequent administrations.

After the Cold War, the sustaining of casualties further declined.[250] The U.S. public and elites became increasingly sensitive to losses.[251] The wider public longed for the peace dividend in the wake of the 1990-91 war, while fussy elites assumed that no strategic purpose could possibly justify the spilling of blood. This fact accounts for America's refusal to take up arms in southeast Europe and to deploy ground troops in humanitarian interventions. In the 1990s, the U.S. government enhanced the standoff capability of its forces to increase their ability to use force without suffering casualties. Since the early 1920s, the air force could use force effectively without the risk of losing soldiers.

In sum, Americans are more likely than Germans to use military force to pursue national interests and political goals. The U.S. technological advantage makes warfare acceptable to many because it minimizes casualties, but a deeply rooted aversion to casualties makes the U.S. reluctant to deploy ground forces.

After World War II, the U.S. could no longer enjoy its security free ride. American security culture shifted from the territorial boundaries on the continent toward global influence and security interests. The U.S. developed a new national security ideology and foreign policy based on the perception of the post-war world and Amer-

---

[248] In the final analysis, the American army is not so much an arm of the executive branch as it is an arm of the American people; see General Weyand quoted in Harry G. Summers, Jr., *On Strategy: A Critical Analysis of the Vietnam War* (New York: Dell Books, 1982), 33.

[249] Farrel, "Strategic Culture and American Empire," 9.

[250] Harvey M. Sapolsky and Jeremy Shapiro, "Casualties, Technology, and America's Future Wars," *Parameters* (Sept. 1996), 119-127; Charles Moskos, "Grave Decision: When Americans Accept Casualties," *Chicago Tribune*, December 12, 1998, 25.

[251] Indeed, the recent Powell doctrine emphasizes the use of overwhelming force to reduce casualties while achieving victory sooner. For information on Powell doctrine see Nicolaus Mills, *The new Killing Fields: Massacre and the Politics of Intervention*, (New York: Basic Books, 2002), 71-88.

ica's place within it.[252] The intent to withdraw U.S. troops from Europe after the defeat of Nazi Germany was soon abandoned with the shift to the new national security ideology. Given the perceived unprecedented Soviet ideological and military threat, the U.S. military could not "simply pack its bags and go home before organizing the West."[253] The new ideology demanded a permanent program of preparedness and vigilance, and facing the Communist threat.[254] It made clear that freedom and peace are indivisible.[255] Thus, through extended deterrence the West European countries became the outposts of America's national defense to "provide for the common defense" and "obtain the blessings of liberty."[256] To reconstruct war-shattered Europe, the U.S. developed several plans to rebuild western Europe—economically through the Marshall Plan, militarily through NATO—as an outer line of defense and to roll back the Communist threat.[257]

During the Cold War, different administrations and the American public defined U.S. interests worldwide. They believed that American security must not be defended at the U.S. coastlines, but in

---

[252] The internationalist foreign policy and a supportive program of state making challenged such traditions as isolationism, antimilitarism, and antistatism; see Michael J. Hogan, *A Cross of Iron: Harry S. Truman and the Origins of the National Security State 1945-1954* (New York: Cambridge University Press, 1993), x. The U.S. made political commitments on the Eurasian continent based on a new strategic idea, the idea of containment; see Dueck, 82.

[253] Harper, 187.

[254] Payne, 64.

[255] The conviction that peace and freedom are indivisible seemed to leave the American people with little choice but to defend their own security and their own liberty by defending peace and freedom everywhere; see Hogan, 14.

[256] Thomas Risse-Kappen, *Cooperation among Democracies: The European Influence on U.S. Foreign Policy* (Princeton, Princeton University Press, 1995), 79.

[257] In June 1947, the Marshall Plan created the general conditions for economic and social recovery of Germany and thus Europe. After the threat that Greece and Turkey might become the next satellites of Soviet imperialism, the Truman Doctrine granted all states military and economic support to remain independent in order to roll back Communism. The U.S. feared the domino effect if the Communists took over Greece or Turkey. See Hogan, 15. During the Berlin crisis of 1948 the threat became even more evident. For roll back, see also Dueck, 85. For Cold War strategy see Lind, *The American Way of Strategy*, 110-124.

Berlin and Taipei.[258] To inhibit communism, George F. Kennan introduced the concept of containment, which used American power to react to Soviet expansionism worldwide.[259] America became the protector and provider "of all those they deemed threatened by a communist takeover"[260] and the hegemon within NATO.[261]

In order to pursue its global interests and security needs, the U.S. acceded to multiple international organizations. The end of World War II was the beginning of the transatlantic link between Western Europe and the U.S. in security affairs; multiple security institutions under American leadership were created worldwide.[262] The United States and Great Britain, at that time the strongest advocates for an international system based on international law, were at the lead in creating the United Nations and the legal order surrounding it.[263] Following the dramatic post-war events in Europe, the necessity of a defensive alliance became evident.[264] After much hesitation, even the U.S., "with its historical antipathy to alliances," accepted the establishment of NATO and its Art. 5 collective defense clause.[265] The

---

[258] Georg Schild, "Amerikas Aussenpolitischer Pragmatismus," *Aussenpolitik* 46, no.1 (Quartal 1, 1995), 33.

[259] Based on Kennan's containment concept, National Security Council Report 68 (NSC-68) was written. Kennan emphasized multiple approaches of foreign policy, while NSC-68 called for military action and preparedness and thus extensive peacetime military spending. The NSC-68 also cited America's historic mission to spread the blessings of liberty on a global scale; see Hogan, 15.

[260] The U.S. support flights during the Berlin crisis accounted for the protection and help towards Western Europe; see Petra Goedde, *GIs and Germans: Culture, Gender and Foreign Relations, 1945-1949* (New Haven: Yale University Press, 2003), 195.

[261] With MC/48, the Europeans transferred the power to start a war to the American president and to some extent to the American military commanders; see Robert S. Jordan, *Norstad: Cold War NATO Supreme Commander: Airman, Strategist, Diplomat* (New York: St. Martin's Press, Inc., 2000), 88.

[262] Risse-Kappen, 19.

[263] Farrel, "Strategic Culture and American Empire," 9.

[264] Greece, Turkey, and Norway, poised to come within the Soviet sphere of influence, the Czechoslovakia coup in 1948 and the Berlin crisis in the same year, all cried out for a Western defense alliance.

[265] Ian Q. R. Thomas, *The Promise of the Alliance: NATO and the Political Imagination* (Lanham: Rowman and Littlefield, 1997), 12.

Washington Treaty in 1949 was based on the principles of the UN Charter. NATO has been perceived as an anchor for security both in Europe and the U.S. Throughout the Cold War, "U.S. leadership had been exercised primarily through NATO."[266] That said, proposals by the U.S. would be supported or opposed by the allies. Most importantly, the allies could be sure of the lead and substantive expertise of alliance operations.[267]

The Korean war became the first manifestation of alliance cooperation in crisis. Since the U.S. saw Europe as its main area of interest and its "outpost of [U.S.] national defense" it refrained from escalating the war into China and shifted its foreign policy towards the European interests.[268] The Korean war proved that the U.S. political leaders, including Truman, Acheson, Eisenhower and Dulles, believed strongly in the European allies and the necessity of the Transatlantic Alliance.[269] The Suez Crisis of 1956 was perceived as another cornerstone of alliance (non-)cooperation. The U.S. felt deceived by its allies' failure to conform to the "fundamental collective understandings constituting the transatlantic community—'trust and confidence.'"[270] The Suez crisis proved that multilateral conformity benefits the international actor and more important, that the U.S. is willing and able to act unilaterally with "coercive behavior" against its allies.[271]

The importance of organizational structure and multilateralism in international organizations decreased in U.S. foreign policy in the 1980s, changing how the U.S. enters and conducts wars.[272] How-

---

[266] James Gow, *Triumph of the Lack of Will, International Diplomacy and the Yugoslav War* (New York: Columbia University Press, 1997), 202.

[267] Jenonne Walker, "Keeping America in Europe," *Foreign Policy*, 83 (Summer, 1991), 129.

[268] Risse-Kappen, 42.

[269] Risse-Kappen, 77.

[270] Risse-Kappen, 96.

[271] Risse-Kappen, 101.

[272] The Defense Recognition Act (Goldwater-Nichols) in 1986 increasingly sidelined the service chiefs as major players in shaping U.S. strategy, doctrine and operations; see Farrel, "Strategic Culture and American Empire," 7; see also Schild, 34.

ever, U.S. participation in international organizations like the UN and NATO and cultural, financial, and economic globalization prevents a complete resumption of the isolatist tradition of American foreign and security policy. Moreover, U.S. administrations have not favored complete decoupling. The strategic concept of forward defense was jettisoned at the end of the Cold War, and the U.S. would "not be able to maintain the same level of commitments in Europe as it had in the past."[273] The Bush administration's foreign policy toward Europe saw the U.S. as leading through NATO, with the Europeans bearing a greater share of the security burden.

In summary, the U.S. has adjusted its position in the post-Cold War world.[274] America's security culture prior the Balkan wars consisted of three predispositions that informed the use of force: technological fetishism and casualty aversion, and multilateral conformity and legitimacy.[275]

B.   U.S. PREDISPOSITIONS AND EARLY PERCEPTION OF THE WAR

Because the impact of the changed international environment prior the outbreak of the Bosnian war on U.S. security culture can not be neglected, this section guides the reader through the early Balkan wars, examines Washington's perception of the Bosnian war, and analyzes the impact of the war on U.S. predispositions. A certain amount of overlap in the subsequent discussion cannot be avoided because the relevant predispositions of U.S. public and political elites are closely interrelated.

America's technological fetishism, decisive warfare and casualty aversion are responsible for the perception of the Balkan wars, along with its orientation toward the new world order, absorption

---

[273] Steven Hurst, *The Foreign Policy of the Bush Administration: In Search of a New World Order* (New York: Cassel, 1999), 210.

[274] Gow, 202.

[275] The author has added multilateral conformity and legitimacy to the list because the multilateral compatibility of U.S. foreign policy seemed more important before the Balkan wars. For the other dispositions see Farrel, "Strategic Culture and American Empire," 8.

with events after 1989, multilateralism, and the relationship with the Yugoslav state.

1. Predispositions and Perceptions Caused by U.S. Domestic Policy

Within a month after the Cold War ended, the Bush administration was focused on how to encourage the peaceful revolution in Central and Eastern Europe. The end of the U.S.-Soviet rivalry that dominated global politics for nearly half a century "presented [Washington] with both a challenge and an opportunity."[276] The opportunity was to shape a new world order which underlined the "validity of the principles which had sustained U.S. foreign policy for the previous forty years."[277] The new world order created a swell of optimism in the U.S.[278] But it also caused fierce debate and criticism of Bush.[279] Washington was overwhelmed by the ramifications of the Soviet collapse and its foreign policy could hardly keep pace with the international and diplomatic revolution. The new U.S. role was still being identified at the outbreak of the Balkan wars. Contributing to the instability and uncertainty was the issue density of different events which drew America's attention, such as the Gulf crisis and the Yugoslav war of dissolution.

The universality of values reflecting American idealism remained intact, which became evident from the support for German

---

[276] The challenge was managing this fundamental transformation, and the prize was to shape a peaceful, prosperous, democratic international system in accordance with the values and interests of the United States; see Hurst, 1.

[277] Hurst, 2.

[278] Bush said in a joint session of Congress that the world will be freer from the threat of terror, stronger in the pursuit of justice, and more secure in the quest for peace; see Gow, 184.

[279] The main criticism was that Bush could not provide a broader vision for U.S. foreign policy. The basic goals of U.S. foreign policy remained exactly what they had been during the Cold War, worldwide economic capitalism with the U.S. as dominant actor; see Hurst, 8.

reunification and the operation in Kuwait.[280] But the Balkan wars proved that idealism had its limits. Although the outbreak of the Balkan wars threatened the values of the new world order, America's "vital interests were not immediately at stake."[281]

The Bush administration was aware of the emerging crisis in Yugoslavia.[282] The American ambassador in Belgrade, Warren Zimmermann, warned the administration in 1990 that the dissolution of the Yugoslav state was a possibility because of the unwillingness to compromise in Yugoslav politics.[283] Secretary of State James Baker voiced deep concerns after his visit in Belgrade in June 1991. Although Belgrade never got U.S. approval to keep the Yugoslav integrity, Baker insisted during his visit that "the United States continues to recognize and support the territorial integrity of Yugoslavia."[284] Nevertheless, on his return to Washington, Baker was more than glad to withdraw from the Yugoslav turmoil. He felt burned by his visit to Belgrade, a city he perceived as a can of worms that the U.S. should avoid.[285] However, Congress began to press hard for a stronger U.S.

---

[280] Stephen F. Szabo, *Parting Ways: The Crisis in German-American Relations* (Washington D.C.: Brookings Institution Press, 2004), 55.

[281] Serbia, as James Baker wrote, did not have the military power of Iraq and it did not threaten the West's oil supplies; see Hurst, 213.

[282] Observers such as Lawrence Eagleburger and Brent Scowcroft who had served in Belgrade had already interpreted the Albanian student revolt of 1968 and the Croat Spring in 1971 as signals of growing ethnic tension. Both voiced their concerns about instability in Yugoslavia; see Rafael Biermann, "Back to the Roots: The European Community and the Dissolution of Yugoslavia – Policies under the Impact of Global Sea-Change;" Christoph Schwegmann, "The Contact Group and its Impact on the European Institutional Structure," *Occasional Papers 16*, Institute for Security Studies, Western European Union, Paris, 31; Hurst, 213; Gow, 204.

[283] Biermann, 47.

[284] Mark Almond, *Europe's Backyard War: The War in the Balkans* (London: Mandarin, 1994), 48-49. It is arguable whether Milosevic perceived the Baker statement as a green light for the Serb intervention in Croatia and Slovenia, but the Serb President felt that the international costs were bearable; see V.P. Gagnon, Jr., "Ethnic Nationalism and International Conflict: The Case of Serbia," *International Security* 19, no. 3 (Winter 1994), 160; Payne, 172.

[285] For the comments by Zimmerman; see Maud S. Beelman, "Hear No Evil, See No Evil: Early U.S. Policy in Yugoslavia", *APF Reporter* 18, no. 1,

involvement. The increasingly emotional political discourse played a role here, stirred up by media reporting on the ground. Senator Robert Dole argued before the Senate that "the United States urgently needs to review its policy toward Yugoslavia" and the United States should "get off the sidelines. We cannot be spectators."[286]

The lessons of Vietnam were raised in the political discourse concerning the Persian Gulf and Bosnia.[287] Intervention in the Balkan wars would have led the U.S. government down a path to a nebulous outcome in terms of military casualties and financial investments. The complexity and intensity of the Balkan wars denied a clearly predictable American victory. Unlike the Persian Gulf, where clear skies and desert terrain favored decisive U.S. operations, the Balkans are cloudy, mountainous and heavily forested.[288] Front lines where U.S. technological superiority would be advantageous were not clearly identified. Still, in 1992 the President stated that he did not want to be involved in guerilla warfare in Yugoslavia because the U.S. had "lived through that once already."[289] Military commanders, with their deeply rooted casualty aversion, recommended that American troops not be involved in the Yugoslav war. They interpreted the conflict as insoluble, whatever the international interventions.[290] In sum, political and

http://www.aliciapatterson.org/APF1801/Beelman/Beelman.html, accessed 27 Apr. 2007. Washington believed that the U.S. would face two international problems if it led any operation in Yugoslavia: first, the international perception and second, the aversion to the U.S. playing the world's policeman; see Gow, 204. "The refusal of the Bush administration to commit American power early was our greatest mistake of the entire Yugoslav crisis;" Warren Zimmermann quoted in Richard C. Holbrooke, *To End a War* (New York: Random House, 1998), 27.

286 U.S Senate, Committee on Foreign Relations, "Civil Strife in Yugoslavia: The United States Response," *Hearing before the Subcommittee on European Affairs, 102nd Congress,, 1st Session,* February 21, 1991, 36-42.

287 Jack S. Levy, "Learning and Foreign Policy: Sweeping a Conceptual Minefield," *International Organization* 48, no. 2 (Spring 1994), 279.

288 Payne, 183.

289 *New York Times,* August 8, 1992, A4.

290 Gert Krell, "Wie der Gewalt widerstehen? Konfliktintervention und die Frage legitimer Gegengewalt als ethisches und politisches Problem," *Der Krieg in Bosnien und das hilflose Europa / Plädoyer für eine militärische UN-Interveation*, Hessische Friedens- und Konfliktforschung, 1993, 14.

military elites perceived that any intervention in the Balkan wars could not end swiftly with a decisive battle and thus would cause American casualties. The Vietnam syndrome was revived.

Also, America and Yugoslavia were perceived to be divided by a cultural distance. Kennan, a former ambassador to Yugoslavia, described its population as a non-European civilization with non-European characteristics.[291] Americans saw the Muslim population in Bosnia as "others." This was reinforced by the growing perception that Muslims threaten the U.S. and the "assumption that Islam is essentially inconsistent with democracy" and therefore incompatible with American values.[292] That said crisis prevention in Yugoslavia in order to diffuse democratic norms would not be at all fruitful. The U.S. initially perceived the Balkan wars as a mix of "aggression, ethnic assertion, self-determination and state preservation. "[293] The hypothesis that "atrocity is natural to the Balkans" added to American assumptions that distant cultures are more prone to violent behavior.[294] Much-read among the Bush Administration was the book "Balkan Ghosts" by Robert D. Kaplan, which saw the wars caused by deep-rooted "ancient hatreds" that could hardly be stopped.[295] The possibility that these wars might have been stirred up by ethnic entrepreneurs was in these days still hardly discussed. Americans saw the outbreak of violence in distant cultures as unfortunate but unavoidable "and beyond America's ability to alleviate."[296] Internationalist foreign policy and support for state building based on the one world concept as a feature of security culture were thus seen as impractical.

Overall, the distinct cultural features of casualty aversion and the emphasis on decisive short battles based on technological advantage biased Washington against forceful early intervention in the

---

[291] Kennan quoted in Payne, 166.

[292] Payne, 170.

[293] Gow, 202.

[294] William Pfaff, "Invitation to War," *Foreign Affairs* 72, no. 3 (Summer 1993), 97-109.

[295] Robert D. Kaplan, Balkan Ghosts: a journey through history (New York: St. Martin's Press, 1993).

[296] Payne, 167.

Balkan wars. The cultural distance to Yugoslavia outweighed American idealist notions of state building and the spread of democracy. Contributing to those predispositions is the fact that American interests during the outbreak of the war were not immediately at stake.

2. Predispositions and Perceptions Caused by the International Environment

The end of the Cold War struck the United States like a tidal wave.[297] The State Department stopped referring to the Soviet Union as an enemy in 1989 with the Bush administration's development of a coherent policy towards the Soviet Union and the Central Eastern European (CEE) states.[298] Transformation of the U.S.-Soviet relationship was the main focus of American foreign policy and issues concerning Yugoslavia could not be isolated from the relationship. The new world order called for the quick development of new foreign policy doctrines and the reorientation of the responsibilities of the last remaining superpower. The cultural dimension of conflict in the Balkans revitalized Russian interest in the Slavic Serbs and directly affected the U.S.-Russian relationship. German reunification was another central issue.[299] The U.S. and the Russians were the strongest and most influential proponents on the German question. German reunification was seen as an integral part of the new world order. The Balkan wars with its refugee problems were perceived as a threat to the new European order.

International organizations provided the primary guidelines for U.S. foreign policy at the outbreak of the Balkan wars because American interests were not much at stake. The U.S. tends to react unilaterally and forcefully when it cares about a problem but is other-

---

[297] Robert M. Gates, *From the Shadows: The Ultimate Insider's Account of Five Presidents and How They Won the Cold War* (New York: Simon and Schuster, 1996), 449.

[298] Woodward, *Balkan Tragedy: Chaos and Dissolution after the Cold War*, 150, 399.

[299] Hurst, 60.

wise willing to rely on others.[300] Thus, American predispositions at the outset of the war have to be viewed through the lens of international organizations.

The Balkan wars presented the U.S. with the problem of maintaining the principle of multilateralism and most importantly, "the unity of the Atlantic Allies."[301] Unlike the Gulf war, in which European allies relied on American military and political capabilities, the Balkan wars were seen as a European crisis that could be resolved without U.S. support. European hubris drove the U.S. away from the Balkan crisis, which was somewhat welcomed by Washington. Significant restraints in handling the crisis resulted from the tensions between the U.S. and the Europeans.

The development of a European security identity in 1990 would have fit perfectly into the Cold War structure of NATO.[302] Yet, after the Cold War, the U.S. perceived the drive for a European security identity outside of NATO and the Eurocorps, a multinational formation developed by France and Germany, as threats. With the Soviet threat vanished, the Bush administration favored strengthening the European pillar in order to reduce its European obligations. But the preferred forum to do this was NATO.[303] The U.S., however, knew that when they share a burden, allies want more of a say in decision-making.[304] Thus, U.S. multilateralism was challenged and torn between contradictory aims.

The problem was that several Europeans, especially France and increasingly Germany, preferred the Western European Union

---

[300] During the Gulf crisis, the U.S. expected its allies to conform to the conduct of the intervention. During most of the Balkan wars, Washington conformed to its European allies and international organizations; see Payne, 187. A stark contrast to the Balkan wars multilateralism is the 1994 diplomatic and military activities in Haiti, where refugees and the proximity to the U.S. put American interests immediately at stake; see Vitas and Williams, eds., 246.

[301] Hurst, 213.

[302] Thomas, 169.

[303] Bush said that the United States remained a power in Europe and that NATO is the key organization in Europe; see Nuechterlein, 193.

[304] Hurst, 220.

(WEU) to strengthen the European capacity to act. but as part of the WEU, Europeans could "seek to distance themselves from American leadership and undermine NATO."[305] The French vision of a more autonomous Europe based on the WEU caused severe friction between NATO members. The agreement on the European Security and Defense Identity (ESDI) within NATO and the concept of Combined Joint Task Forces (CJTFs) in 1994 was a compromise, after the EU had started to formulate its own Common Foreign and Security Policy (CFSP) in Maastricht in 1991 already.[306] This inevitably imposed on the unwilling Americans both "a far more 'European' alliance than had previously existed"[307] and the perspective of a separate European defense pillar outside NATO.

This was the background for U.S. early action when the breakdown of Yugoslavia occurred. On the one hand, the Bush administration favored a hands-off policy, perceiving this as a European affair. On the other hand, it feared to loose too much control. Thus, once the fighting started in Slovenia and then Croatia, the Bush administration responded with concern about both the option of recognition and the leading role of the Europeans.[308] It was irritated by the new European assertiveness and realized how little it could now influence the European recognition debate, which ran counter to U.S. preferences. The Balkan wars thus tested the American principles of multilateralism and burden sharing.[309]

The success of the operation to liberate Kuwait "cast a shadow over subsequent U.S. policy on Yugoslavia."[310] The Persian Gulf

---

[305] Thomas, 169.

[306] The French vision of the ESDI was to sideline NATO and undermine U.S. leadership in Europe. The U.S. and British intention was that the WEU become an adjunct to and not a replacement for NATO; see Thomas, 169.

[307] Anand Menon, *France, NATO and the Limits of Independence 1981-1997: The Politics of Ambivalence* (New York: St. Martin's Pree, Inc., 2000), 59-60.

[308] Hurst, 215.

[309] Hurst, 215. "It was time to make the Europeans step up to the plate and show that they could act as a unified power. Yugoslavia was as good a first test as any." James Baker quoted in Holbrooke, 28.

[310] Gow, 203.

crisis of 1990-91 created an opportunity for the U.S. to reorient its foreign policy.[311] Iraq's invasion of Kuwait helped clarify the U.S. government's view of its role in the international order. The Gulf war was seen as the model for the new world order. Domestically, the U.S. operation received heavy criticism.[312] The success of the U.S. operation gave Bush substantial support in the elections, but the war also exhausted Washington.[313] Presidential advisors were reluctant to endanger the likely electoral success by involvement in the Balkans, where no U.S. interests seemed to be at stake.[314] The Gulf war exemplifies clearly defined perceptions of good and evil, unambiguous moral choices and clearly identified American interests.[315] The perception of the Bosnian war was exactly the opposite.

Yugoslavia had a special relationship with the West motivated by the geostrategic and political rationale directly connected to the Truman doctrine that Soviet client states that follow the Yugoslav example of splitting from the Soviet Union would receive political and financial support.[316] The U.S. firmly supported the unity, territorial integrity, and independence of Yugoslavia and later the initial transition to democracy and a free market.[317] Its privileged position

---

[311] Hurst, 126-127.

[312] Bush was criticized because he neglected diplomatic and economic efforts, relied on the use of force and abandoned the operation too early. See Hurst, 86.

[313] "Even a great power has difficulty in dealing with more than one crisis at a time." Warren Zimmermann quoted in Holbrooke, 26.

[314] Klaus Larres, "Bloody as Hell," in *Journal of European Integration History* 10, no. 1 (2004), 186.

[315] In the 1970s, oil became the vital economic interest of the U.S.; see Nuechterlein, 203.

[316] The geostrategic motivation was to prevent Yugoslavia from drifting back into Soviet hegemony and to block Soviet influence in the Adriatic Sea. The political motivation was to promote a viable alternative to the Soviet client states; see Biermann, 37. Yugoslavia played a critical role for U.S. global leadership as an integral element of NATO's policy in the eastern Mediterranean; see Woodward, *Balkan Tragedy: Chaos and Dissolution after the Cold War*, 25; Holbrooke, 24; Biermann, 38.

[317] Yugoslavia had long enjoyed Most Favored Nation trade status (MFN) with the U.S. and was the ninth largest user of the Generalized System of Preferences (GSP), which ensures duty-free access for exports to the U.S.

gave Yugoslavia a free ride until 1991 with regards to its human rights record.[318] With support from the U.S., the EC became Yugoslavia's main partner.[319] At the end of the Cold War, Washington saw the Balkans as lying outside the U.S. "sphere of interest."[320]

Principled idealism and isolationism were the traditional U.S. foreign policy impulses early in the conflict.[321] But the U.S. still tried diplomatically to prod the Europeans into stronger action and later returned to a multilateral initiative as a way of spreading responsibility. In July 1991, the administration warned in a NATO meeting in Brussels that Milosevic "needed to be stopped if a bloody break-up of Yugoslavia was to be avoided."[322] Europeans in NATO, especially Great Britain and France, replied that the events in Yugoslavia should not be over dramatized. On a CSCE meeting on minority rights in July 1991, the U.S. delegation was "frustrated about the unwillingness of the Europeans even to mention internal affairs, particularly human rights abuses."[323] In November 1991 at the NATO summit in Rome, the U.S. put heavy pressure on the Europeans and emphasized that "attempts to change existing borders through the use of force or a policy of fait accompli are unacceptable."[324] But Washington accepted the lead of the European Community mediating the early conflict. One consequence was that it also had to accept the EC fait accompli of recognizing Croatia and Slovenia in early 1992, which undercut

---

[318] Biermann, 38.

[319] Biermann, 38.

[320] Larres, 151.

[321] Gow, 185.

[322] Biermann, 47.

[323] Biermann, 45.

[324] Hurst, 216.

U.S. foreign policy goals and was highly criticized.[325] Washington later had to follow the Europeans and recognize the secessionist states.

In sum, the international environment, including multilateral obligations, rules and norms imposed by international organizations had an obvious effect on U.S. foreign policy. The U.S. lent its support to international organizations because vital American interests seemed not to be at stake. Washington wanted the Europeans to take most of this burden. The U.S. was predisposed to act with caution and avoid upsetting Russia, whose transformation was Washington's main concern.

C.   THE IMPACT OF THE BOSNIAN WAR

This section guides the reader through the Bosnian war. It links aspects of the war, as the independent variable, with culture bearing units in the U.S., representing the security culture; it analyzes public opinion and political discourse. This section is divided into three subsections. The first explains the transmittance of the Bosnian war to America and the importance of means of communication. The following two subsections examine the change of U.S. foreign policy towards Bosnia. They will demonstrate a change in the rating of cultural preferences and analyze the repercussions during the later years of the war.

Because Yugoslavia was outside Washington's sphere of interest, America reacted slowly to the war. Clinton's election in 1993 did not immediately change policy toward Bosnia, although Clinton's rhetoric in the campaign was quite interventionist. American foreign policy involved multilateral operations that constrained their operations in Yugoslavia. Washington was busy preventing the conflict from spilling over to neighboring countries, delivering humanitarian aid to Bosnian minorities, and putting increasing economic and dip-

---

[325] The U.S. saw the interaction of the economic and political crises in Yugoslavia and sent economic assistance to avert political destabilization. The reform program of Ante Markovic, who personally enjoyed great sympathy in the U.S., was paramount for international assistance. Throughout early 1991, the U.S. administration backed Markovic and tried to maintain the Yugoslav state through negotiations; see Biermann, 39; Hurst, 214; Gagnon, 149, 153.

lomatic pressure on Serbia. The continued ineffectiveness of UN and European mediation forced the Clinton administration to take action. Washington finally intervened in the conflict because the credibility of NATO and the U.S. both were at stake; but the change of U.S. foreign policy was caused by a reorientation of America's own interests. The international deadlock in Bosnia plus increasing domestic pressure made a new political course of action possible in the summer of 1995. The insight grew that America was still more needed than expected in Europe, that NATO was gliding into a serious identity crisis without going "out-of-area". The U.S. had to remain an active player in Europe and world affairs. Thus, American foreign policy changed to actively assume responsibility for resolving the conflict, a change that finally resulted in the contribution of 20,000 U.S. troops to keep the peace after the Dayton agreement.

1. The Role of the Media in the U.S.

The United States is a paradise for media and the press. As Biagi notes, "[I]n no other country do the mass media capture so much of people's time and attention."[326] Washington, D.C. is home to the White House, the cabinet departments, and Congress along with other places where newsworthy information is made public every day.[327] Endless briefings, statements and hearings with images and international news are made public through the media. The media was a decisive causal link between the Bosnian war and U.S. foreign policy. The "relentless coverage" of inhumane acts, the siege of Sarajevo, and Bosnian war victims were linked to a variety of U.S. policy responses and "reflect causation rather than coincidence."[328] Most reporters lived in Sarajevo, as did the war's most frequent victims. Their articles and broadcasts "influenced public opinion and fed the moral exasper-

---

[326] Shirley Biagi, *An Introduction to Mass Media* (Toronto: Thomson Wadsworth, 2005), 4.

[327] Jonathan Mermin, *Debating War and Peace: Media Coverage of U.S. Intervention in the Post-Vietnam Era* (Princeton: Princeton University Press, 1999), 17.

[328] Larry Minear, Colin Scott, and Thomas George Weiss, *The News Media, Civil War, and Humanitarian Action* (Boulder: Lynne Riener Publishers, 1996), 3.

ation among academics, legislatures, and senior policymakers."[329] During the hostage crisis in May 1995, the world's press was invited by the Bosnian Serbs to film "human shields" handcuffed to trees and telephone poles. The world saw broadcasts of miserably humiliated UN peace keepers and French soldiers waving white flags.[330] Those pictures did not deter the American public, but rather provoked support for the UN to "get tougher."

One-time Speaker of the U.S. House of Representatives Thomas "Tip" O'Neill famously claimed that "all politics is local." He meant that politicians working on a global stage are influenced by their electorate.[331] In fact, public opinion is an important element in American security policy decisions. Some scholars even believe that "opinion polls are at the core of presidential decision making."[332] Others argue that when presidents "go public" they can garner support to convince fellow politicians and Congress.[333] Hence, public opinion becomes a political tool. For this reason, American politicians pay close attention to opinion polls both as a tool and to manipulate political goals. American administrations hype the threats of the belligerents when going to war. In Operation Desert Shield in Kuwait, the Bush administration became very concerned about public opinion.[334] When the media showed pictures of American hostages held in Iraq, Bush gave the hostage issue and Iraq's alleged nuclear weapons program greater prominence to gain public support and justify the use of force. Normally there is broad public support when the President

---

[329] Evelyn N. Farkas, *Fractured States and U.S. Foreign Policy: Iraq, Ethiopia, and Bosnbia in the 1990s* (New York: Palgrave MacMillan, 2003), 122.

[330] Holbrooke, 64.

[331] Sabine Collmer, "'All politics is local': Deutsche Sicherheits- und Verteidigungspolitik im Spiegel der Oeffentlichen Meinung," in *Deutsche Sicherheitspolitik: Eine Bilanz der Regierung Schroeder*, edited by Sebastian Harnisch, Christos Katsioulis, and Marco Overhaus (Baden-Baden: Nomos Verlagsgesellschaft, 2004), 201.

[332] Richard S. Beal quoted in Ronald H. Hinckley, *People, Polls, and Policymakers: American Public Opinion and National Security* (New York: Lexington Books, 1992), 4.

[333] Samuel Kernell quoted in Hinckley, 5.

[334] Opinion polls in October 1990 showed a slippage of around ten percent in support for Bush's policy in the Gulf; see Hurst, 102.

initiates military action.[335] The public "rallies 'round the flag" when national interests are at stake and military action pursues coherent goals.

The images of the Bosnian war atrocities had mixed impact because the American public generally supports one out of four basic standpoints on foreign policy.[336] American perception of the war was therefore fractured. In addition, the U.S. media is often "systematically selective in reporting international events"[337] or manipulates material to favor some groups. The American public lacks knowledge of international affairs and is thus vulnerable to manipulation. However, a Gallup opinion poll in May 1993 found that about 70 percent of Americans followed the events in Bosnia at least fairly closely.[338]

In America, the impact of the media on the public sphere was not as strong as in Germany. Because other issues absorbed American attention and the media, such as the relationship and the transformation in Russia and the Gulf war, Somalia, and Haiti, Yugoslavia was "simply not on the screen."[339]

2.   The Impact of the Bosnian war

American engagement in the Bosnian war was conspicuously lacking. The U.S. did not participate in the International Conference on Former Yugoslavia, hardly paid attention to it and later sidelined it. It did

---

[335] Dueck, 141.

[336] Eugene R. Wittkopf classifies the American public as isolationists, accommodationists, internationalists and hardliners. See Hinckley, 10.

[337] Hinckley, 133.

[338] To keep informed, the public relies on television and to a lesser extent newspapers. See Gallup opinion research sponsored by CNN and USA Today, May 6, 1993;
http://institution.gallup.com/search/results.aspx?SearchTypeAll=Bosnia&SearchCon Type=1&Place=H, 10, accessed 1 May 2007. Almost 80 percent of Americans said that they were somewhat to very familiar with the events in the Bosnian war; see Steven Kull and Clay Ramsay, *U.S. Public Opinion on Intervention in Bosnia*, Program on International Policy Attitudes, CISSM, School of Public Affairs, University of Maryland, May 15, 1993, 17.

[339] Biermann, 46.

not participate in UNPROFOR. During the first three years, Washington rejected any use of U.S. and NATO forces other than for air strikes and embargo operations which proved to be relatively inefficient. The Bush and Clinton administrations effectively left it up to the Europeans to determine Western policy.[340] The U.S. policy towards the Bosnian war can be best described as fluctuating between the rhetoric about responsibility and reluctance to back those words with military force. In August 1995, the Clinton administration changed course, as taking the lead seemed less risky than other courses of action. American containment and disengagement policy ended with recognition of the fact that engagement was unavoidable.[341]

a.   The Hesitant Superpower

At the start of the Bosnian war in April 1992, the Bush administration was passive, hoping that the UN and Europeans could stop the fighting. Following Europe's diplomatic lead and anticipating EC support, the U.S. advocated expelling Yugoslavia from international organizations, withdrawing the ambassadors and closing American airports to the Yugoslav national airline.[342]

In August, the media began reporting the humanitarian nightmare. Pictures of the atrocities, criticisms of candidate Clinton, the support of various influential politicians and interest groups, specifically American Jewish elites and the diasporas, forced the administration to react.[343] Bush made the Bosnian war "zur Chefsache" (a Presidential concern) to avert the impression that Bosnia was not a political focus.[344] Although initially reluctant, Bush eventually pro-

---

[340] Ivo H. Daalder, *Getting to Dayton: The Making of America's Bosnia Policy* (Washington D.C.: Brookings Institution Press, 2000), 6.

[341] Daalder, *Getting to Dayton*, 63.

[342] James Baker proclaimed that the U.S. will not and cannot be the world's policeman; see Hurst, 216.

[343] Thomas Paulsen, *Die Jugoslawienpolitik der USA 1989-1994* (Baden-Baden: Nomos Verlagsgesellschaft, 1995), 86.

[344] "Chefsache" is the term used by the German Chancellor Gerhard Schroeder to convince people that the Chancellor himself will take control of a situation and respond properly.

posed using air power to enforce a UN Security Council resolution to safeguard humanitarian flights to Sarajevo.[345] Public opinion supported using U.S. forces in UN humanitarian relief efforts. In December 1992, the Gallup organization found that 57 percent of Americans favored the use of U.S. aircraft, while 36 percent rejected it. In February 1993, 68 percent favored participation, and only 29 percent opposed it.[346]

Secretary of State Baker addressed the humanitarian nightmare but claimed that there will be no American use of force.[347] The Bush administration and military leadership feared a protracted conflict with an unclear outcome and American casualties.[348] The President worried that the failure of an American campaign would lead to "calls for the commitment of substantial allied ground forces."[349] In a Congressional hearing the Assistant Secretary of State for European and Canadian Affairs, Thomas Niles drew an indirect reference to the Vietnam war in the minds of military authorities.[350]

The humanitarian situation deteriorated in the winter months. In October 1992, the U.S. threatened to use airpower to enforce the UN no-fly zone over Bosnia. Almost 63 percent of Americans favored the deployment of U.S. aircraft, while 29 percent disagreed. As

---

[345] Larres, 192.

[346] See Gallup opinion research sponsored by Gallup Poll News Service, December 4, 1992;
http://brain.gallup.com/search/results.aspx?SearchTypeAll=Bosnia&SearchConType=1, 11. For February polls see Gallup opinion research sponsored by CNN and USA Today, February 26-28, 1993;
http://institution.gallup.com/search/results.aspx?SearchTypeAll=Bosnia&SearchConType=1&Place=H, 10, accessed 01 May 2007.

[347] Hurst, 217.

[348] Paulsen, 77-80.

[349] Bush said he not want to see the United States bogged down in guerilla warfare in Yugoslavia, the United States having lived through that once already. See "Conflict in the Balkans; Bush says any U.S. Action must come through U.N.", *New York Times*, 8 August 1992, A4.

[350] "Developments in Yugoslavia and Europe," Hearing before the U.S. Congressional Subcommittee on Europe and the Middle East, August 4, 1992 (Washington D.C.: U.S. Government Printing Office, 1993), 8.

during most of the Bosnian war, the public was more willing to employ force and act strongly than the Administration. However, the military leadership refused deployment due to the ill-defined use of force. General Colin Powell was quoted as saying, "decisive means and results are always to be preferred, even if not always possible."[351] In fact, the U.S. Air Force was strongly restricted in how to enforce the no-fly zone. Any use of force had to be multilateral, first authorized by the UN Headquarters in New York, and exerted only for humanitarian purposes, not to resolve the underlying political problem – a procedure that drew rising criticism and caused deep frustration in Washington.[352] The Bush administration thus in late 1992 followed three main principles: no ground forces, military involvement for humanitarian relief only, and the primacy of the UN and the Europeans. Those principles were heavily criticized domestically.

The Bosnian war was seen as involving a vital American interest only if the war spilled into other regions.[353] This position had broad support. In early 1993, only 15 percent of the public thought that national security was a good reason for military intervention in Bosnia; only 16 percent felt that U.S. interests were at stake. The largest reason cited for intervention (37 percent) was to stop ethnic cleansing.[354]

Bush was clearly influenced by candidate Clinton's foreign policy critique.[355] As a campaigner free of policy making responsibility, Clinton supported air strikes and urged military support, strong rhetoric that led Americans to think that foreign policy would change

---

[351] Powell quoted in Paulsen, 99.

[352] Hurst, 218.

[353] Paulsen, 103.

[354] Gallup opinion research sponsored by Newsweek, January 28-29, 1993; http://institution.gallup.com/search/results.aspx?SearchTypeAll=Bosnia&SearchConType=1&Place=H, 10, accessed 01 May 2007; The general argument that intervention should be undertaken due to moral obligations to stop "ethnic cleansing" and to a lesser extend due to U.S interests, is supported in other polls; see Kull and Ramsay, *U.S. Public Opinion on Intervention in Bosnia*, May 15, 1993, 9.

[355] Larres, 193.

if he won office.[356] The public urged the government to take a more active role in the Bosnian war.[357] In an attempt to safeguard the election, Bush announced in a West Point speech in January 1993 that "the United States should not seek to be the world's policeman," adding that "in the wake of the Cold War, it is the role of the United States to marshal its moral and material resources to promote a democratic peace. It is our responsibility – it is our opportunity – to lead. There is no one else."[358]

In the spring, international efforts focused on the Vance-Owen Plan. The U.S. thought that diplomatic options had eroded after a Bosnian Serb attack on Srebrenica on March 18.[359] After further Serb aggression, the U.S. pushed through monitoring of the no-fly zone with Operation Deny Flight, the start of NATO involvement. The Clinton administration opted for an even stronger NATO commitment in a "lift and strike" strategy in May 1993. "Lift and strike" meant lifting the arms embargo on Bosnia and using U.S. and NATO air strikes to attack Serb strongholds. At the opening of the Holocaust Museum in late April, Clinton was deeply impressed by Elie Wiesel's comparison of ethnic cleansing in Bosnia with the Holocaust. In talks

---

[356] In January 1993, the Gallup institute found that 24 percent of Americans thought it very likely that U.S. troops would be send to Bosnia and 38 percent believed that it was likely. While 44 percent thought that the President was very likely to support operation deny flight, 38 percent thought that it was likely. See Gallup opinion research sponsored by Newsweek, January 14-15, 1993;
http://institution.gallup.com/search/results.aspx?SearchTypeAll=Bosnia&SearchConType=1&Place=H, 11, accessed 01 May 2007. See also Daalder, *Getting to Dayton*, 6.

[357] In January 1993, 55 percent of Americans favored the deployment of U.S. forces to Bosnia in a multilateral effort, while 41 percent opposed it. The public notion towards casualty aversion was ambivalent. While 41 percent sought that the involvement of U.S. troops would end up like the Vietnam war, 47 percent believed in a Gulf War outcome; see Gallup opinion research sponsored by CNN and USA Today, January 24-26, 1993;
http://brain.gallup.com/search/results.aspx?SearchTypeAll=Bosnia&SearchConType=1, 10, accessed 27 Apr. 2007.

[358] George H. W. Bush, Address at the West Point Military Academy, United States Military Academy, West Point, NY, January 5, 1993.

[359] Daalder, *Getting to Dayton*, 12.

with Polish and Czech political leaders, Clinton saw NATO's future threatened by the Bosnian war. Lech Walesa and Vaclav Havel argued that their states were in a vacuum since the Soviet collapse; they wanted to join NATO and needed U.S. support. Washington's reluctance to deal with the Bosnian war was contrary to the hopes of the CEE governments. These considerations led Clinton to accept the "lift and strike" strategy.[360]

An April poll found that 62 percent of Americans would oppose and only 30 percent would favor unilateral U.S. air strikes against Serb strongholds. A month later, the public favored the strikes.[361] Support for a multilateral effort was at 59 percent.[362] When the option of intervention with ground troops was described as a unilateral American action, public support averaged 43 percent, but multilateral action garnered 60 percent support.[363]

Secretary of State Warren Christopher could not persuade the European allies to back the "lift and strike" strategy.[364] The Europeans would only accept to the "lift and strike" strategy in the Bosnian question with more pressure and a definite commitment of Washington.[365] Europe feared that U.S. unilateral actions like those taken in the Suez crisis would damage the Alliance; furthermore they feared an increasing influx of weapons into the region with lifting the arms embargo and thus saw the security of their own troops in UNPROFOR at stake. On the other hand, Washington was unwilling to lead inter-

---

[360] See Ronald D. Asmus, *Opening NATO's Door: How the Alliance Remade Itself for a New Era* (New York: Columbia University Press, 2002), 23-25.

[361] In May, 55 percent opposed and 36 percent favored the U.S. air strikes against Serb strongholds. See Gallup opinion research sponsored by CNN and USA Today, May 6, 1993;
http://institution.gallup.com/search/results.aspx?SearchTypeAll=Bosnia&SearchContType=1&Place=H, 8, accessed 01 May 2007.

[362] Kull and Ramsay, *U.S. Public Opinion on Intervention in Bosnia*, May 15, 1993, 1.

[363] Kull and Ramsay, *U.S. Public Opinion on Intervention in Bosnia*, May 15, 1993, 1.

[364] The allies, specifically Great Britain and France, had ground forces in Bosnia and feared that NATO air strikes against Serb strongholds would threaten them; see Larres, 198.

[365] Daalder, *Getting to Dayton*, 17. The only way to make the Europeans agree to the U.S. preferred strategy was the raw power approach; see Asmus, 22.

national crisis management.[366] Thus Clinton dropped the "lift and strike" idea and returned to diplomatic placebos.

Washington adopted the European idea of containment, defending six Muslim enclaves that had been declared safe areas by the UN.[367] Allied requests for troops for Bosnia were neglected by Clinton.[368] In May 1993, he promised financial support for the Arms Export Control Act to enforce sanctions against Serbia and Montenegro, and for humanitarian aid to Bosnian and Croatian refugees. Clinton changed his rhetoric and emphasized that financial support served America's national security interest.[369]

In July, the deteriorating humanitarian situation again made headlines. After feverish discussion, the administration again pushed for "air power in the service of diplomacy."[370] This time Washington threatened to proceed unilaterally and the European allies voiced support, although they forced compromises that resulted in the infamous "dual-key" arrangement, which so much undermined NATO/US-UN relations.[371] In October 1993, President Clinton first said that the U.S. had "significant interests" in resolving the Bosnian

---

[366] President Clinton was criticized due to the ""lift and strike"" strategy. The chances to get the approval through Congress were 'point blank zero;' see Paulsen, 128.

[367] Daalder, *Getting to Dayton*, 18.

[368] Clinton met the allied request with the harsh response that he would not send American troops into a "shooting gallery;" see "Remarks of the President in a Photo Opportunity with the Cabinet," White House, Office of the Press Secretary, May 21, 1993.

[369] See Presidential Determinations 93-20, May 3, 1993 and 93-22, May 19, 1993; quoted in Vitas and Williams, 252.

[370] Daalder, *Getting to Dayton*, 20.

[371] The U.S. wanted full control of air strikes by the commander of Allied Forces South (AFSOUTH). In the "dual-key" arrangement, air strikes would only be requested (and could also be vetoed) by military on scene commanders. They had to be approved by the UN and NATO after the latter proved their feasibility. See Thomas R. Mockaitis, *Peace Operations and Intrastate Conflict, The Sword or the Olive Branch*, 97. Since the on scene commanders were French and British soldiers, the Europeans had an enormous leverage over the air strikes. See Daalder, *Getting to Dayton*, 23.

conflict, a statement that led to a heated debate in Congress.[372] The majority of Congress opposed the deployment of ground forces. Military leaders were concerned about the troop deployment and argued that the complex Bosnian war was not comparable with the war in Iraq.[373] Gallup in May found that 68 percent of Americans favored deployment of U.S. troops to achieve peace in Bosnia.[374] In October, with the unfolding of the crisis in Somalia, Clinton became more aware of risk, and public support for sending troops to Bosnia dropped to 40 percent.[375]

Overall, public support for unilateral American action was weak, but multilateral efforts got stronger support. A growing consensus within political elites and the public called for something to be done. Opinion polls revealed steadily increasing support for multilateral military intervention and the use of force. Instead of acting unilaterally, the Clinton Administration preferred NATO entanglement in the war. The American discourse slowly shifted from purely humanitarian considerations to concern for U.S. national security and U.S. interests.[376]

---

[372] See Clinton's Letter to the Senate Leaders on the Conflict in Bosnia in Vitas and Williams, 253; General-Anzeiger, 05 May 1993, 4.

[373] Frankfurter Rundschau, 30 July 1993, 2.

[374] See Gallup opinion research sponsored by CNN and USA Today, May 6, 1993; http://institution.gallup.com/search/results.aspx?SearchTypeAll=Bosnia&SearchConType=1&Place=H, 9, accessed 01 May 2007.

[375] See Gallup opinion research sponsored by CNN and USA Today, October 08-10, 1993; http://institution.gallup.com/search/results.aspx?SearchTypeAll=Bosnia&SearchConType=1&Place=H, 8, accessed 01 May 2007.

[376] Kull and Ramsay, *U.S. Public Opinion on Intervention in Bosnia*, May 15, 1993, 18-19.

b.   Engaging Diplomacy

In January 1994, pressure on the United States increased.[377] Madeleine Albright, the U.S. Ambassador to the UN, voiced deep concerns about America's Europe policy and the credibility of NATO.[378] In February, Walter B. Slocombe urged members of the U.S. House of Representatives to remain engaged in NATO and to press forward to bring peace, prosperity and democracy to the new Europe.[379] The necessity for U.S. leadership was made manifest by political elites.

The artillery shelling of the Sarajevo marketplace on February 5 unexpectedly catalyzed U.S. policy. Broadcasted images of the 68 dead and 200 wounded civilians caused widespread aversion in America. In the wake of the attack, NATO imposed a strict ultimatum on the Bosnian Serbs to lift the siege and backed it with a threat of air strikes.[380] Sixty-five percent of Americans favored air strikes.[381] The same poll revealed that 32 percent saw involvement in the Bosnian war as in the U.S. interest, while 59 percent claimed there were other

---

[377] Paulsen, 161-163. In January, NATO allies pressured the U.S. to deploy ground forces to Bosnia. Polls showed that 27 percent of Americans favored the deployment, while 68 percent opposed it; see Gallup opinion research sponsored by CNN and USA Today, January 6-8, 1993,
http://institution.gallup.com/search/results.aspx?SearchTypeAll=Bosnia&SearchC onType=1&Place=H, 8, accessed 01 May 2007.

[378] Amerika Dienst 7, 16 Feb. 1994, 2; Daalder, *Getting to Dayton,* 24.

[379] Walter B. Slocombe, testimony before the House of Representatives, Committee on Foreign Affairs, Subcommittee on Europe and the Middle East, Committee on Armed Services February 2, 1994,
http://web.lexisnexis.com/congcomp/document?_m=cef13802cca1c198e06c0860f 3fa31da&_docnum=1&wchp=dGLbVlb-
zSkSA&_md5=e76d7f98062cfb9ad6ae12fc518977e3, accessed 06 May 2007.

[380] The Americans and the French agreed on a heavy weapon exclusion zone of 20 kilometers around the enclaves; see Daalder, *Getting to Dayton,* 24; Paulsen, 164-165.

[381] See Gallup opinion research sponsored by CNN and USA Today, February 7, 1994,
http://institution.gallup.com/search/results.aspx?SearchTypeAll=Bosnia&SearchC onType=1&Place=H, 8, accessed 01 May 2007.

reasons to get involved. After the Sarajevo bombing, even support for the deployment of combat troops went up.[382]

The diplomatic initiative by Clinton and the Germans, the Washington Agreement, brokered a peace between the Bosnian and Croat forces, reducing the belligerents to two.[383] Additionally, the U.S. and Russia found a compromise to deal with the Krajina region at Zagreb.[384] The Clinton administration's diplomatic offensives were the first successful initiatives in the Bosnian war, although the initiative was counter to the efforts of the ICFY, because the belligerents hoped to gain more from direct contact with America.

In April 1994, the Contact Group was formed as the main forum of the external parties, partly because the U.S. resisted working with David Owen and Thorvald Stoltenberg, the joint Chairmen of the ICFY.[385] Instead of a multilateral approach with all twelve governments of the European Union or the EU Troika, the U.S. wanted close dialogue with the members of the UN Security Council, including Germany, but outside of New York.[386] European and U.S. diplomats were convinced that close cooperation was the only practical way to settle the Balkan conflict. Unlike former peace plans, the emerging Contact Group plan had a distinct American signature. It

---

[382] In February 1994, 35 percent of Americans favored deployment of U.S. troops to enforce peace in Bosnia, while 57 percent opposed. One month later, 41 percent favored and 53 percent opposed troop deployments. More than 60 percent perceived the atrocities of the Bosnian Serbs comparable with the Holocaust. See Gallup opinion research sponsored by CNN and USA Today, March 11-13, 1994, http://institution.gallup.com/search/results.aspx?SearchTypeAll=Bosnia&SearchContType=1&Place=H, 7, accessed 01 May 2007.

[383] Daalder, *Getting to Dayton,* 26; Paulsen, 167-168.

[384] Russia had demonstrated its influence on the Bosnian Serb forces in February 1994 by persuading them to withdraw their heavy artillery from the Sarajevo mountains. The Z-4 Plan, brokered by the U.S. and Russia as a compromise solution on the Krajina, was not accepted by the opposing parties. See Christoph Schwegmann, "The Contact Group and its Impact on the European Institutional Structure," *Occasional Papers 16,* The Institute for Security Studies Western European Union, Paris, June 2000, 4.

[385] Schwegmann, 4.

[386] Greece, which held the EU presidency, followed a Yugoslavia policy at odds with that of the U.S. and contrary to U.S. interests. See Schwegmann, 4.

was presented to the belligerents as a non-negotiable take-it-or-leave-it proposal.[387]

American public opinion in April showed between 76 and 81 percent favoring NATO air strikes to stop attacks on Bosnian cities. Almost 73 percent supported an American role in a UN peacekeeping force to enforce a peace agreement. Even without a peace settlement, almost 66 percent favored contributing to UN peacekeeping operations in Bosnia. An overwhelming 90 percent supported UN peacekeepers using force to deliver humanitarian aid.[388]

Washington tried to persuade its allies once more to accept a "lift and strike" strategy. This time, however, Clinton asked for unilateral termination of the arms embargo in case the Security Council "fails to pass such a resolution."[389] This raised strong concerns among the allies. The Danish Permanent Under Secretary of State for Defense, Anders Troldborg, told a Congressional hearing in June that NATO solidarity must be maintained, warning of disruption to the alliance if the U.S. tried to lift the arms embargo unilaterally.[390]

In November 1994, the Republicans, led by Senator Robert Dole, a long-time advocate for active intervention, captured the Congress.[391] Congressional pressure and the successful offensive of the Croat troops in May 1994 to re-conquer Western Slavonia and Smyrnia, thereby overrunning UNPROFOR, encouraged the Clinton administration once more to consider of lifting the arms embargo uni-

---

[387] Schwegmann, 5.

[388] Steven Kull and Clay Ramsay, *U.S. Public Attitudes on U.S. Involvement in Bosnia*, Program on International Policy Attitudes, CISSM, School of Public Affairs, University of Maryland, May 4, 1994, 1.

[389] President Clinton's letter to the Chairman of the Senate Committee on Armed Services on the Arms Embargo on Bosnia-Herzegovina: see Vitas and Williams, 254-255.

[390] Permanent Undersecretary of State for Defense, Denmark, Anders Troldborg, Testimony before the United States Senate, Committee on Armed Services, June 23, 1994,
http://web.lexisnexis.com/congcomp/document?_m=e628c39860e9ee22271d7c4f ab6bd561&_docnum=2&wchp=dGLbVlb-zSkSA&_md5=74de5399eac201954e5f2950265fc0d3, accessed 06.May 2007.

[391] Daalder, *Getting to Dayton*, 31; Larres, 200.

laterally.[392] Moreover, the upcoming election pushed the administration to follow public opinion and increase political pressure to end the war. Opinion polls revealed a gradual decline of sympathy for the Clinton policy.[393] Yet, in October 1994, 45 percent of Americans believed that vital U.S. interests were at stake in Bosnia. Two-thirds of Americans believed that it would be best for the U.S. to take an "active part in world affairs."[394]

Overall, public opinion in 1994 showed a steadily increasing support for American involvement in the Bosnian war. Most Americans supported American involvement in a multilateral effort to settle the conflict. The willingness to use force in a multilateral effort, e.g. air attacks on Serb strongholds, increased enormously.

c.   *Exercising Leadership*

In 1995, the Bosnian war took on a new dimension. Newly elected French President Jacques Chirac agreed with Washington and favored massive air strikes against the Bosnian Serb strongholds. In February, the Security Council asked NATO to plan for the withdrawal of UN-

---

[392] In fact, the U.S. Senate gave an ultimatum to the Clinton administration to lift the arms embargo. Washington was encouraged by the offensive of Croat proxy forces to get militarily involved; see Larres, 200.

[393] In late February 1994, 42 percent approved of Clinton's policy, while 43 percent disapproved. This declined gradually to 31 percent approval and 48 percent disapproval in July; for February polls see Gallup opinion research sponsored by CNN and USA Today, February 26-28, 1994, for July polls see Gallup opinion research sponsored by CNN and USA Today, July 15-17, 1994,
http://institution.gallup.com/search/results.aspx?SearchTypeAll=Bosnia&SearchConType=1&Place=H, 6-7, accessed 01 May 2007.

[394] John Rielly quoted in Ivo H. Daalder, "Prospects for Global Leadership Sharing: The Security Dimension," in: *Maryland/Tsukuba Papers on U.S.-Japan Relations* edited by I.M. Destler and Hideo Sato, Center for International and Security Studies at Maryland (CISSM) School of Public Affairs, July 1996, 37.

PROFOR.[395] In April, polls showed that the public was frustrated with UNPROFOR but only 29 percent of Americans wanted the UN to withdraw from Bosnia. The majority favored more forceful UN intervention and the deployment of third-party military forces.[396] On the other hand, the public opposed unilateral circumvention of the arms embargo.[397] Washington said it would contribute U.S. forces to protect UNPROFOR if they were to withdraw from Bosnia. Even as the U.S. tried to discourage UN withdrawal, it "offered the solution to the administration's predicament."[398]

When UN blue helmets were taken as hostages by the Bosnian Serbs, this was the moment of either to withdraw or to upgrade engagement. Great Britain and France began to deploy additional ground troops as a Rapid Reaction Force (RRF) to support UNPROFOR.[399] William J. Perry, the U.S. Secretary of Defense, stating

---

[395] UN Secretary General, Boutros Boutros-Ghali has called for a serious reevaluation of the entire UN peacekeeping operation in Bosnia; see Steven Kull, *Americans on Bosnia: A Study of US Public Attitudes Summary of Findings*, Program on International Policy Attitudes, CISSM, School of Public Affairs, University of Maryland, May 16, 1995, 1; The Pentagon and NATO completed OPLAN 40104, a planning document that covered every aspect of NATO's role in supporting a UN withdrawal; see Holbrooke, 66.

[396] 50 percent of Americans favored a tougher intervention of the UN forces and more than 87 percent favored the use of force when aid convoys are attacked or obstructed. 65 percent voiced to defend civilians in safe havens and 64 percent favored following through on a UN threat to intervene with a large military force to stop ethnic cleansing with the participation of 50,000 to 100,000 U.S. troops; see Steven Kull quoted in Daalder, "Prospects for Global Leadership Sharing: The Security Dimension," 39-40.

[397] Only 16 percent of all respondents favored the unilateral lift of the arms embargo; see Kull, Americans on Bosnia: A Study of US Public Attitudes Summary of Findings, 6.

[398] With UNPROFOR (and thus French and British forces) gone, the U.S. could lift the arms embargo and conduct air strikes without opposition; see Daalder, *Getting to Dayton*, 93.

[399] Daalder, *Getting to Dayton*, 163. The RRF was deployed to galvanize a diplomatic, political, economic, and military endgame in the conflict; see Lantis, *Strategic Dilemmas and the Evolution of German Foreign Policy since Unification*, 116.

clearly that the U.S. would not provide own troops.[400] Yet, support to the RRF was broad. In a Congressional hearing in mid-June, James Schlesinger concluded his comments with the words, "original peace keeping is now over – finished!"[401] The UN was more and more gliding from peace keeping into peace making.

After an initial four month cease-fire, fighting in Bosnia erupted with new intensity. Americans were once again "confronted with troubling images of indiscriminate attacks on civilians and helpless UN peacekeepers."[402] In July, media attention focused on the conquests of Srebrenica and Zepa, UN safe havens. Polls showed 68 percent of Americans favoring defense of civilians in safe havens.[403] The American public and elites were overwhelmed by the pictures of the July 6 Srebrenica massacre.

---

[400] Perry did not believe that the Bosnian war posed a threat to U.S. interests grave enough to risk the lives of thousands of U.S. troops. There was no support among the public or in the Congress for entering the war as a combatant. He opposed the commitment of ground forces. But he also clearly stated that under the following conditions the U.S. might envision sending ground troops to Bosnia: First, as part of a NATO force to help implement a peace settlement, if one is reached and second, as part of a NATO force to help the UN forces withdraw. American support, he argued, could make a key difference, as it had in NATO. The goal of the administration was to protect U.S. interest in the Balkan region—not a vital national security interest, but an interest in European security, limiting violence, and the flow of refugees. See William J. Perry, testimony before the Senate Armed Services Committee, June 07, 1995,
http://web.lexisnexis.com/congcomp/document?_m=9df70afa4f349727df39e8a1b
e69ffc6&_docnum=12&wchp=dGLbVlb-
zSkSA&_md5=5f2b6f998a01f07e4605483bf9bc844b, accessed 06 May 2007.

[401] Schlesinger argued that U.S. forces should support the withdrawal of UN-PROFOR, saying that when allied forces are in trouble, they count on America. See James Schlesinger, testimony before the Committee on Armed Services, United States Senate, June 15, 1995,
http://web.lexisnexis.com/congcomp/document?_m=9df70afa4f349727df39e8a1b
e69ffc6&_docnum=7&wchp=dGLbVlb-
zSkSA&_md5=ad4770354b4ac53f31f9714fd8e85205, accessed 06 May 2007.

[402] Kull, *Americans on Bosnia: A Study of U.S. Public Attitudes,* Summary of Findings, 1.

[403] Kull, *Americans on Bosnia: A Study of US Public Attitudes Summary of Findings,* 2.

In the summer of 1995, with a presidential campaign pending, four factors pushed the Clinton administration to engage in the Bosnian war and reclaim leadership in NATO.[404] The four factors were the loss of UN credibility after the Srebrenica massacre, the threat to NATO's legitimacy and thus relevance, the prospect of U.S. troop deployment and the Congressional vote to lift the arms embargo. If the U.S. let the moment slip away, Clinton claimed, America would be "history."[405] Sensing that a policy window had opened, he reconsidered Bosnia policy, backed by Madeleine Albright, Anthony Lake and after the Srebrenica massacre by William Perry.[406] The North Atlantic Council (NAC) members called the Bosnian Serb attacks unacceptable and threatened NATO use of force. After the European allies agreed to the new strategy, and with continuing Serb attacks on safe havens, the NAC decided to use air power.

The U.S. affirmed its lead role by acknowledging that NATO was responsible for the safe withdrawal of UNPROFOR. The U.S., which agreed to deploy ground forces to support the withdrawal, insisted that command and control be shifted from the UN Secretary General to the United States.[407] To facilitate air attacks, the Commander-in-Chief Southern Europe (CINCSOUTH) and the Commander UNPF signed a memorandum of understanding on the execution of air strikes in August 1995. Three weeks later, CINCSOUTH and Commander UNPF decided to launch air strikes in Operation Deliberate Force, supported by the U.S. Navy.[408] Operation Storm in August, the startling Croatian re-conquest of the Krajina, was a blow to the Bosnian Serbs, who saw the Croats army now moving forcefully into Northern Bosnia and changing the balance of power on the ground. For NATO, this was an enormous boost, not only solving

---

[404] Daalder, *Getting to Dayton*, 165.

[405] Daalder, *Getting to Dayton*, 166.

[406] The new course of action, known as the endgame strategy, aimed to establish a military balance in Bosnia by lifting the arms embargo and arming and training the Bosnian forces, all secured by air strikes during the transition period. See Daalder, *Getting to Dayton*, 166-172.

[407] Woodward, *Balkan Tragedy: Chaos and Dissolution after the Cold War*, 398.

[408] Holbrooke, 103.

most of the Croat problem before Dayton but also changing the power distribution in the Bosnian war in favor of the Bosnian Croat federation and demonstrating that the Serbs can indeed be defeated by determined force.[409] In September, the Bosnian Serbs accepted a peace process which was followed by a cease fire in mid-October and negotiations on the Dayton agreement led by U.S. envoy Richard Holbrooke.

Opinion polls in September showed 52 percent of Americans favoring deployment of U.S. troops in a peace keeping force, while 43 percent opposed. Polls in October revealed that aversion to American casualties remained strong. When the same question was posed with a hypothetical 400 U.S. soldiers killed, only 20 percent favored a deployment; 72 percent were against it. Even with only 25 hypothetical American casualties, 64 percent of the public said they would oppose deployment.[410] However, the public perceived the intervention as an operation comparable to the Iraq war rather than a Vietnam-style quagmire. Thus in October, public opinion changed to favor deployment. Optimism rose as the war came to an end. Almost 80 percent of Americans perceived peaceful developments in Bosnia as a U.S. foreign policy goal. Over half—54 percent—saw U.S. intervention in Bosnia now as a moral obligation to stop atrocities perpetrated by the Bosnian Serbs. Forty-two percent supported the reasoning that U.S. leadership in the world required the American troop deployment, and 35 percent believed that it was a U.S. vital interest to engage in the war.[411]

---

[409] The Croat offensive in Krajina profoundly changed the nature of the Balkan game and thus the U.S. diplomatic offensive according to Joe Kruzel, a member of the Holbrooke team. Cited in Holbrooke, 72-73.

[410] See Gallup opinion research sponsored by Gallup Poll News Service, October 19-22, 1995,
http://institution.gallup.com/search/results.aspx?SearchTypeAll=Bosnia&SearchConType=1&Place=H, 4, accessed 01 May 2007.

[411] Sixty-eight percent of Americans favored and 29 percent opposed deployment. See Gallup opinion research sponsored by Gallup Poll News Service, October 19-22, 1995,
http://institution.gallup.com/search/results.aspx?SearchTypeAll=Bosnia&SearchConType=1&Place=H, 4, accessed 01 May 2007.

In September 1995, the U.S. Senate adopted an amendment which expressed the sense of the Senate on prior approval for deployment of U.S. ground forces in Bosnia and Herzegovina by an overwhelming vote of 94 to 2.[412] In a subsequent Congressional hearing, Secretary of Defense Perry claimed that if a peace agreement is reached, it is essential that the United States and its NATO allies, along with our international partners, be prepared to sustain that negotiated peace. As the alliance responsible for peace and security in Europe, NATO can do no less. As the leader of NATO, the United States must lead and shape this effort—an action necessary to protect vital national interests.[413]

To summarize, the Clinton administration's change of course was caused by the escalating agony of the war and its appalling humanitarian suffering, by the failure of EU and UN to end the war in the International Conference on Former Yugoslavia diplomatically and through UNPROFOR on the ground, by the increasing threat to NATO's relevance, by the changing power balance on the ground through the Croat offensives, by the prospect of U.S. troop deployment and by the Congressional vote to lift the arms embargo. The change was backed by broad support from the general public and political elites, support that increased continuously after the Bosnian Serb attacks on safe havens.

3.   Pax Americana

William Perry has said that "history has demonstrated the consequences of instability in Europe. If the U.S. does not commit itself in

---

[412] This was the so-called "Gregg Amendment." U.S. Senate, 104th Congress, 1st session. In September 29, 1995;
http://web.lexisnexis.com/congcomp/document?_m=80b6aa1b5edc88677347182f
a5bd991b&_docnum=1&wchp=dGLzVlz-
zSkSA&_md5=fd2e78c6a73883094dcd6e078837826b

[413] Secretary of Defense William J. Perry and Chairman of the Joint Chiefs of Staff, General John M. Shalikashvili, testimony before the House Committee on National Security and House Committee on International Relations, November. 18, 1995, http://web.lexisnexis.com/congcomp/document?_m=b2ea4f746710a632492e3234
c421baf7&_docnum=1&wchp=dGLbVlb-
zSkSA&_md5=984e427e16d841fb9d20b3e46c89413d, accessed 06 May 2007.

Europe, it will rue the consequences for the long term security of Europe and for its own security."[414] The Dayton Peace Accords were a defining moment not only for Bosnia, but in international politics.[415] The agreement has been called a "Pax Americana," as the major negotiations were conducted by the U.S. delegation under Holbrooke.[416] The breakthrough was possible because of NATO's bombing of the Serb strongholds and because of the renewed U.S. diplomatic leadership.[417]

The NAC authorized the Supreme Allied Commander in Europe (SACEUR) to deploy an enabling force into Bosnia-Herzegovina on December 1, 1995. The SACEUR tasked the CINCSOUTH as Commander for the Implementation Force (IFOR). A few days later, Secretary of State Christopher claimed that the President had decided that the U.S., as a world leader committed to peace keeping, should "act as the great nation," with a concern for both national interests and American ideals.[418] Clinton justified the U.S. action after the Dayton Agreement as promoting both American values and Washington's interest in a world order with a stable Europe. With its fragile new democracies adjacent to America's closest allies, "Europe's freedom and Europe's stability is vital to [America's] own national securi-

---

[414] Secretary of Defense William J. Perry on the deployment of U.S. troop with the Bosnia Peace Implementation Force before the House Committee on International Relations, November 30, 1995,
http://web.lexisnexis.com/congcomp/document?_m=e6283bc0c68497c1c1761a16
e926376f&_docnum=2&wchp=dGLbVlb-
zSkSA&_md5=222fc219ab54558db612f8022358b4cc, accessed 06 May 2007.

[415] Gow, 1.

[416] Schwegmann, 6.

[417] European Union negotiator Carl Bildt claimed that the breakthrough was caused by the Clinton administration's decision to back a peace initiative with robust military means; see Schwegmann, 7.

[418] Warren Christopher, testimony before the U.S. Senate, December 6, 1995,
http://web.lexisnexis.com/congcomp/document?_m=3cd4951ff9faf1624a3d95f23
8cd4184&_docnum=8&wchp=dGLbVlb-
zSkSA&_md5=23a3e1a495c3db4474e2e53c8179b820, accessed 06 May 2007.

116

ty."[419] While the Bosnian war did not harm America's view of the world order, the promotion of values was a vital interest of the U.S.[420]

Surveys in December found that 71 percent felt strongly about the presence of American troops in Bosnia.[421] There was also widespread opposition in the U.S. government against a military entanglement.[422] IFOR was led by NATO under U.S. command, as was the Stabilization Force (SFOR) one year later.[423]

D.   CONCLUSION

Comparison of the dispositions of U.S. administrations and American society before and after the Bosnian war shows no significant difference. Yet, the Bosnian war did challenge the core elements of American security culture: multilateral conformity, casualty aversion, and technology fetishism and commitment to decisive war. Distinctive cultural features framed the U.S. response to the Bosnian war. The administrations gradually moved to align themselves with public opinion; the Bush administration's non-intervention gave way to humanitarian and eventually military intervention under Clinton.

The element of multilateralism did not change during the Bosnian war. Reliance on international organizations, especially NATO, was central to U.S. foreign policy throughout the war. The

---

[419] Promulgating American values and vital interests, the President then described the instrument he would use to settle the Bosnian conflict, namely NATO. If the Americans were not in Bosnia, NATO would not be there either. Bill Clinton cited in Nuechterlein, 242.

[420] Nuechterlein, 244.

[421] See Gallup opinion research sponsored by CNN and USA Today, December 15-18, 1995, http://institution.gallup.com/search/results.aspx?SearchTypeAll=Bosnia&SearchConType=1&Place=H, 4, accessed 01 May 2007.

[422] In July 1995, Lawrence Eagleburger referred to Bosnia as "another part of the world." In November, Senator Phil Gramm claimed that all of Bosnia was not worth one American soldier. See Michael A. Sells, *The Bridge Betrayed: Religion and Genocide in Bosnia* (Berkeley: University of California Press, 1996) 124, 128.

[423] Schwegmann, 9.

Bush and the Clinton administration kept to the multilateral approach and tied the use of force to multilateral legitimacy. American foreign policy was compatible with organizational norms and rules and with international obligations. Throughout the war Washington consulted European allies, worked toward its policy goals through international organizations, and accepted compromises. A major reason for this was that Washington could thus shift the burden to others without committing itself more than necessary. Even after the war, the majority of Americans envisioned the possible deployment of American troops as part of a multilateral force, rather than in a unilateral intervention.[424] Moreover, Americans opposed even diplomatic unilateral actions like lifting the arms embargo. Although American adherence to multilateral norms is recognized as compromising effectiveness and decisiveness, during the Bosnian war it left a mark on American perception of multilateralism.

However, the Yugoslav crisis revealed the limitations of the EU and the UN in accepting a larger burden.[425] The European principals of those institutions were unable to carry the burden of European security alone, and the U.S. was forced to take more responsibility than anticipated. Americans who hoped to put the principles of multilateralism and burden-sharing into practice saw that the time was not ripe for the European allies and international organizations to take all the responsibility for Europe.[426] The Europeans could not build up a credible military threat to avert or contain the war, a threat that becomes necessary when nonviolent approaches fail.[427] Thus, Europe's leading role, a major concern of the Bush administration, became problematic. Eventually the U.S. had to regain its leadership role in NATO.

The cultural features of casualty aversion and the emphasis on decisive short battles and technological advantage also did not change during the Bosnian war. The American administrations followed a

---

[424] Richard Sobel and Eric Shiraev, eds., *International Public Opinion and the Bosnia Crisis* (New York: Lexington Books, 2003), xii.

[425] Hurst, 239.

[426] Hurst, 215.

[427] Craig and George, 259.

consistent foreign policy line. With the "lift and strike" strategy, Washington tried to repeal the arms embargo imposed by the UN early in the conflict, with parallel air strikes to stop the atrocities. The U.S. hoped that this strategy could change the military balance and thus stop the fighting. In the meantime, Washington hoped the decisive use of airpower would prevent violence and carnage. The "lift and strike" strategy was consistent with casualty aversion and the emphasis on decisive warfare.[428] Since deployment of American ground forces would have led to a nebulous outcome in terms of military casualties, the administration favored lifting the arms embargo and strengthening the Bosnian and Croat armies as proxy forces. On the other hand, political and military elites were aware that intervention with ground troops would not end the war swiftly with a decisive battle, since the war's complexity and intensity defied clear victory. Thus, the elites relied on the American and NATO's technological advantages in the form of air strikes. America's reliance on air power and proxy forces proves its continued preference for limited liability.[429]

According to Dueck, American strategy in the Bosnian war was marked by "intense reluctance to back up [the] internationalist agenda by force."[430] The case study of the Bosnian war shows that this reluctance is consistent with the security culture of the United States. The lack of enthusiasm for involvement in Bosnia was challenged throughout the war by the American public. The Clinton administration was forced to back its policy with military pressure in late 1994 when NATO's credibility was at stake. Thus the Bosnian war became more central for U.S. interests than originally perceived in

---

[428] The military leadership did not perceive the air strikes as decisive warfare, since the "dual-key" arrangement hindered any effective decisive operation. The U.S. negotiators were urged by American NATO leaders to prevent an agreement between the civil administration in Bosnia and Herzegovina and the military command. The U.S. military feared the civilian influence on military operations which proved to be problematic during the "dual-key" arrangement between the UN and the U.S. which neglected decisiveness. Thus, in late 1995 the conducts of air strikes were controlled solely by CINCSOUTH.

[429] Dueck, 139.

[430] Dueck, 137.

1992. In June 1995, when the war threatened the credibility of the U.S. as a European power, the Clinton administration persuaded the allies to accept an endgame strategy.

The research shows that the majority of Americans supported the use of force even when there was no threat to vital American interests.[431] The support for air strikes against Serb strongholds had almost tripled by April 1994. Most Americans supported deploying U.S. troops in a multilateral force after a peace agreement was established. Fewer favored the deployment of forces without a peace agreement, which would be a deployment to enforce peace rather than to simply monitor it. However, when faced with the prospect of American casualties, support for U.S. military deployments declined, especially after the Somalia operation. Polls show that Americans wanted the UN to "get tougher" and a majority favored deployment of U.S. troops in a multilateral force if UNPROFOR was harassed while fighting ethnic cleansing. That said, Americans perceived the Bosnian war as comparable to Iraq, rather than Vietnam, and favored the use of overwhelming force to stop the humanitarian disaster in Bosnia. Political and military elites, even more strongly averse to casualties, supported a policy which relied on technological advantage and minimized American casualties. Even strong advocates of American intervention in the Bosnian war like Senator Robert Dole did not envision sending ground forces.

Eventually, the United States came to realize that "European problems in the realm of security were American problems."[432] Throughout the Bosnian war, America's role in the post-Cold War era was still unclear. The issue density of different international events kept America's attention focused on domestic politics and on relations with Russia and trouble spots like the Gulf, Somalia and Haiti. America's retrenchment from international responsibility was danger-

---

[431] The widespread desire for intervention was prompted largely by humanitarian and other normative considerations. American interests were implicated only broadly in preventing the war from spreading. See Steven Kull and Clay Ramsay, "U.S. Public Opinion on Intervention in Bosnia" in *International Public Opinion and the Bosnia Crisis,* edited by Sobel and Shiraev, 69.

[432] Woodward, *Balkan Tragedy: Chaos and Dissolution after the Cold War,* 398.

ous for international security, especially where there was a need for decisive use of military force.[433] The Bosnian war proved that in the mid-1990s, the alternative to American leadership was no leadership. The complex and unprecedented security challenges of the Bosnian war required leadership. The prospect of a highly competitive security environment compelled the U.S. to engage the Bosnian war in order to help manage European security.[434] The Bosnian war was a catalyst for the U.S. to identify its new or rather rediscover its old role in Europe, a matter not of changes in security culture, but of practical and consistent reorientation of foreign policy.

---

[433] Daalder, "Prospects for Global Leadership Sharing: The Security Dimension," 41.

[434] Daalder, "Prospects for Global Leadership Sharing: The Security Dimension," 42.

VI. GERMAN SECURITY CULTURE AND U.S. INTERESTS

The Bosnian war clearly demonstrates the relevance of culture for international politics. The diplomatic and strategic revolution of 1989 challenged both world politics and theories of International Relations. Also, the increasingly shared security culture among transitional actors in the post-Cold War era required a rethinking and reorientation of international relations. Euro-Atlantic security cultures adjusted to the post-Cold War environment.

The Bosnian war has been an enduring political shock experience with far-ranging repercussions on German and U.S. society and political elites alike. The war unfolded as a series of formative events understood as individual incidents with singular but interrelated impacts (e.g. the continuous shelling of Sarajevo and the attacks on Srebrenica). The density and duration of the Bosnian war increased the intensity of its effect. At the time, the sheer amount of destruction, ethnically motivated atrocities and displacements complicated attempts to understand this intra-state war in a new era that started out with hopes to have banished nationalism, ethnic hatred and war.

The war's profound and challenging issue density and duration increased its impact on Germany and the U.S, especially as it stood in stark contrast to the perceived new world order. The main transmitters were the media, personal visits to Bosnia, the refugees and their lobbying as diaspora communities and the reporting of human rights organizations. They transported the war into Western societies and thus mediated between the war and domestic security cultures. Formative events spurred international condemnation. Equally striking is the effect of the war as a whole. Major intervening variables that exposed the public and elites to the war include personal experiences in the war zone and exposure to the war through mass media. In addition, the testimony of refugees contributed to the transmittance of the war in Germany. The 350,000 refugees who sought asylum in Germany presented a large scale refugee crisis. Those refugees were human rights violations made visible. The Bosnian war was perceived as a humanitarian crisis by American and German publics and elites.

This thesis has explored the security cultures of Germany and the United States during the Bosnian war, beginning in 1992 and ending with the Dayton Peace Accords of 1995. Case studies of both Germany and the U.S. have demonstrated that security cultures influence the assessment of political situations, restrain policy objectives, and condition the range of issues to which political attention is devoted. The German case study reveals that the security culture indeed changed profoundly, primarily as concerns the use of force. This change affected the evaluation of available policy options and the decisions about using German military force outside territorial defense and treaty obligations. The case study of the U.S. likewise reveals that security culture predisposes foreign policy behavior; however, in contrast to Germany, when faced with the same events, a strong security culture does not necessarily change. Yet the U.S. case study shows that distinct cultural features, a ranked set of grand strategy preferences, were adjusted during the war in favor of a more pronounced leadership role in the complex security challenges of the post-Cold War era.

At the beginning of the conflict, German and American politics were quite different; the two nations had almost opposing opinions on the use of force in international crisis management. Germany refrained from any use of military force apart from territorial defense and NATO obligations. Use of force was simply rejected by the elites and by society at large as inappropriate and even taboo. Derived from World War II and the political culture of the Federal Republic of Germany during the Cold War, Germany's distinct cultural features—the foreign policy of responsibility and the culture of restraint—precluded almost all military intervention. This exceptional history led German political elites to deemphasize force as an instrument for achieving national objectives. The political elite was all the more willing to stress that military force was unconstitutional under the nation's Basic Law. As an advocate of soft power, Germany acted diplomatically and only in the background throughout the first phase of the conflict, not committing its forces to UNPROFOR or calling for military engagement.

The U.S. at first refrained from even diplomatic interference after an initial probe prior to the war. Focused on other international trouble spots, the George H. W. Bush administration at first simply did not imagine forceful intervention in European affairs. The distinct cultural features of casualty aversion and technological fetishism did not preclude using force. But the Balkan war was seen as a European affair, and the administration had begun to downplay the relevance of Europe in its geostrategic considerations and to shift the responsibility for European affairs primarily to the Europeans. However, due to the much greater willingness to use force in international conflicts, the policy change towards intervention did not involve a change of the U.S. security culture. Thus, the U.S. repeatedly tried to push the "lift and strike" option through and led NATO into successively assuming more responsibility up to the Air Campaign. However, both Germany and the U.S. adhered strictly to the norms of multilateralism throughout the whole war. German culture demanded that it pursued foreign policy only with multilateral legitimacy. The U.S. followed a multilateral course because they also preferred multilateralism, but also because it conveniently fitted the purpose to shift the burden to the Europeans.

The Bosnian war seemed to stand in contradiction to the new world order and German reunification; German elites thus perceived a vital interest in settling the conflict. In contrast, the war did not initially affect U.S. vital interests. Although German and American interests were affected differently, both nations at first abstained from military intervention and later became fully involved in peace enforcement, taking pivotal roles in the peace settlement and post-conflict peace building phases. This reveals a convergence, not only of policies but also of cultures. German security culture became more like the American culture in terms of how use of force is perceived, whereas U.S. foreign policy shifted towards a more proactive, responsible and leading role in European affairs.

Germany left crisis management to other European states for almost two years after the diplomatic "rapid reaction force" of early recognition. An internal learning process led to questioning the Basic Law and the constitutional legitimacy of the use of German forces. Most importantly, Germany began a process of critical self-reflection.

124

The traumatic impact of the Bosnian war challenged the core beliefs and values of the German public and the political parties. They caused stress because of dissonance within the public and the government. The result was several years of agonizing public debate on the use of force in international politics. Public support for contributing German troops to UN peacekeeping forces remained mixed, yet there was a slow and steady increase of support from about 47 percent in August 1992 to 67 percent in April 1993. Support for contributing troops for UN peace enforcement tripled in the same time period.

America was sidelined by its European allies before the outbreak of the war. The U.S. accepted European leadership in settling the crisis because the war seemed not to affect American vital interests and no core beliefs and values were challenged. The distant Balkan culture was seen as violence-prone. The outbreak of violence in distant cultures was perceived as unfortunate, unavoidable and not within America's power to alleviate. U.S. policymakers believed that crisis management in the Bosnian war could be shouldered by the European allies. However, the humanitarian disaster unfolding since August 1992 spurred a growing consensus among political elites and the general public that "something" should be done. Opinion polls revealed a reluctant but steadily increasing support for multilateral military intervention and the use of force. The government thus endorsed NATO involvement and tried to persuade European allies to accept the "lift and strike" strategy which promised fewer casualties with NATO's technological advantage. The desire for intervention was prompted largely by humanitarian and other normative considerations. American interests were at first only broadly affected by ensuring that the war did not spread. Yet the justification for U.S. intervention shifted slowly from pure humanitarian considerations to concern for U.S. national security and interests, specifically as concerns the viability of NATO.

German political elites, trying to propagate peace but with a strong aversion to using military force, were caught in a dilemma. The logic of the Bosnian war exaggerated this dilemma because peace could only be enforced with military means. The Bosnian war impact was strong and enduring enough to induce great changes in the political attitudes of the German political elite, specifically in respect to the use of military force outside territorial boundaries and the NATO obligations. The war's long duration allowed time for political elites to learn. The distinct cultural features of German foreign policy turned out to be increasingly incompatible with the complex security environment of the post-Cold War era. Environmental feedback in the form of escalating atrocities publicized by the media led to individual learning, followed by individual actions to change the socialized thinking of political parties. Even pacifist groups in Germany were forced to consider the use of military means.

The bombing of Sarajevo and later the Srebrenica massacre finally discredited the core beliefs and values of the German political parties and the general population. The enduring political shock forced a reorientation of beliefs, norms and values which would not have occurred otherwise. The Bosnian war demonstrated the necessity of a totally new approach to intervention and Germany's use of force. It was a period of profound reorientation, self-reflection and rethinking which challenged core beliefs and resulted in a substantial change in the German security culture. The German case study also reveals that the sheer quantity of humanitarian tragedy in the Bosnian war changed the security culture in Germany. The Balkan tragedy created a moral imperative for the public and elites to take action. This action required the utility, quality and quantity of military forces in crisis management.

In 1994, Washington began to see the European problem in Bosnia also as an American problem. The Bosnian war revealed the limitations of UN and EU and their principals. The inability to shoulder the burden of European security and to intervene forcefully in Bosnia decreased their credibility and thus the credibility of NATO and the U.S. as well. Formative events (the siege of Sarajevo, the 1995 post-ceasefire violence, conquests of UN safe havens) increased public support for forceful UN intervention and use of a large scale military force if UNPROFOR was threatened. The November 1994 electoral defeat in Congress further increased domestic pressure on the Clinton administration. Thus, the U.S. government became more and more concerned with a conflict which had entered the U.S. sphere of interest. Increasingly, Washington was concerned about following multilateral rules and norms which often proved to end in a deadlock as strong domestic pressure called for a more forceful and proactive engagement.

Like Germany, Washington was stuck in a dilemma caused by its security culture. On the one hand, Washington adhered strictly to multilateral norms and rules. On the other hand, it followed a strategy of settling the conflict by decisive military means, using technologically advanced air strikes in the hope of minimizing casualties. This culturally inspired new way of war fighting was incompatible with multilateralism, since the European allies for the most part disapproved of air strikes against Serb strongholds. Washington re-ranked its cultural preferences throughout the Bosnian war. Multilateralism dominated during the first years of the war. Though still strong in 1995, the preference for multilateralism lost ground relative to other norms. Washington took the leadership in Bosnian peace enforcement and more or less forced the European allies to accept the enforcement strategy. American diplomatic intervention coincided with other events such as the attacks on safe havens, the UN hostage crisis and the Croat offensive in August 1995. The hostage crisis convinced the Europeans to deploy the RRF and increased pressure to withdraw UNPROFOR. Those events offered a solution to Washington's predicament, and it took a leading role to effectively and responsibly resolve the conflict.

Overall, the Bosnian war had a significant effect on the security culture of Germany and a lesser effect on that of the United States. Germany's "weak" and comparatively young security culture, when confronted with the Bosnian war after 1989, was revealed as vulnerable and Cold War-specific. The complex security challenges after the revolution of 1989 necessitated a rethinking and re-orientation of cultural beliefs and norms. The Bosnian war in particular catalyzed the change of the German security culture. Germany's distinct cultural aversion to the use of force was abandoned and shifted in the direction of the American style of using forces in international crisis management. Thus, the Bosnian war triggered the convergence of German and American security cultures, which is particularly interesting because it contradicts the perceived trans-Atlantic rift.

The "strong" features of the U.S. security culture, entrenched for decades, proved their strength and longevity, but were challenged by the uncertainty and instability of the post-Cold War era. The strategic and diplomatic revolution of 1989 necessitated a redefining of America's role in world politics which was challenged by the uncertainty and instability of the post-Cold War era. America's leadership role in European security affairs was put into doubt at the start of the Bosnian war, but retrenchment from international responsibility presented a real danger in the transitional phase of the early 1990s. Specifically cases that needed decisive use of military force and the will to implement it necessitated U.S. leadership. Washington recognized that the Bosnian war represented a danger to the credibility of NATO and the U.S. The prospects and risks for this highly complex security environment compelled the U.S. to intervene, recognizing that its allies were not able to shoulder the burden of European security. That said the lost confidence in the European allies and the disappointment during the Bosnian war is partly responsible of the trans-Atlantic rift in the early 21st century, as is the US unilateralism in Dayton. Overall, the change in U.S. foreign policy was based not upon cultural change but upon a change of U.S. foreign policy goals and interests.

This thesis has found that German perception of military force changed considerably within a few years, while the cultural preferences of the United States internally shifted as a result of a re-oriented U.S. interest in the international environment. Examination of the Bosnian war and its effect on German and American security cultures demonstrates the impact of crises and political shocks on international actors, the subsequent cultural changes they cause, and the implications this has for policy preferences and behavior.

VII. CONCLUSION

This conclusion integrates the findings of the case studies into the existing framework of security cultures. Some findings augment recent scholarly work, some shed new light on the concept of security cultures, and others raise more questions. The sources of security cultures are addressed first, followed by questions about the static vice dynamic and homogeneous vice heterogeneous nature of security cultures. Finally the aspect of interdependence and multilateralism is addressed.

This thesis agrees with the scholarly findings that material and ideational factors are essential for shaping security cultures, inter alia geography, history and recent experiences, political structure and the institutional framework. Specifically, geography and history are central elements in the security cultures of Germany and the United States. They have a profound effect on these security cultures, cause path dependence, shape and transform them. The geographical granted free-ride with weak neighbors and two oceans around insulated the U.S. from the destruction of the European wars and reduced the perceived imminence of the Soviet threat during the Cold War. Yet, the Cuban Missile Crisis demonstrated how geography could change this security perception. With threats and anxieties comparatively low, optimism could spread as landmark of the strong and self-confident security culture that matured in the United States. In Germany, the predator of two world wars and geographically close to the Warsaw Pact and the Soviet Union, an almost diametrically opposed security culture developed. The unique German historical experience had path dependent effects, caused an extremely cautious, responsible and constrained foreign policy that stood in contrast to the more forceful, pro-active policy the U.S. could afford both due to its history and its status as a superpower.

Both case studies prove that the internal political structure of a state and its institutional entrenchment significantly influence security cultures. The institutional framework, in which both countries operated during the Cold War, considerably impacted their national security cultures, specifically in regard to the perception of human rights. However, the institutional influence was different. As a reluctant, restrained power, Germany saw multilateralism as the only legitimate channel to pursue foreign policy goals. Thus, it allowed the use of military force only in a multilateral framework, and only for territorial defense and treaty obligations. Organizational cultures, especially the integrationist European Community culture, spilled over and shaped the German national security culture. The U.S. also perceived multilateralism as vital to American interests, focusing mainly on NATO as concerns the European outreach. Yet, as the hegemonic power in transatlantic institutions, the U.S. had more leverage in the organizational framework. In other words, the U.S. was able to use the institutional framework to further its own interests and could afford "to got it alone" where preferable. Thus, Washington also pursued foreign policy goals outside the institutional framework, specifically in cases that concerned the American continent. The American leverage proved to be functional insofar as Washington used NATO's military capability to get involved and finally settle the Bosnian war.

Overall, the study proves though that the influence of organizational culture is limited and strongly dependent on the national actor. The U.S. as a hegemonic power with a strong security culture can act outside any organizational culture more than Germany and thus, can shape and influence other national actors and organizations to a considerable extent.

Given that historical memory, recent experiences, and multilateral commitments shape security cultures, it is evident that those cultures and thus foreign policy are in a continuous process of transformation. In the discourse on change of cultures some scholars argue that cultures are persistent, static, and resistant to change; others argue that cultural change is slow and incremental. The latter emphasize that greater dynamism might be triggered by great forces, such as traumatic experiences, crises, and political shocks. The slow incremental change of security cultures is caused by learning through a continuous process of internalization and socialization in which learning conditions later learning. Great changes in direction and velocity caused by traumatic experiences and crises discredit core beliefs and values. Such defining events are critical junctures with a path-

130

dependent effect. Initial policy choices after those defining events determine future policy trajectories and outcomes.

In fact, this thesis reveals that cultures are both persistent and dynamic. The U.S. security culture showed a high degree of stability during the Bosnian war. The strong, centuries-old U.S. security culture mainly persisted in the early 1990s. Yet some cultural features were challenged after the Cold War and specifically during the Bosnian war. German security culture, specifically as concern the use of force, was socially constructed only after WW II, a product of the Cold War. It was thus time-dependent and doomed to be challenged by the new post-Cold War security environment. In other words, the security culture of Germany was not compatible with the new reality after the Cold War and thus started to change, a process which was catalyzed by the Bosnian war. The distinct cultural aversion of the use of force had been internalized and socialized for fewer than five decades and was vulnerable to change. The large-scale humanitarian tragedies in the Bosnian war served as a catalyst for considering policy options beyond the traditional tenets of German security culture.

Whereas the domestic impact of the Bosnian war changed the direction and the transformation velocity of German security culture, a reassessment and re-ranking of cultural preferences took place in the U.S. Multilateralism was discredited and lost ground relative to other cultural preferences. As the U.S. grew more impatient with the entire vector of UN-EU intervention in Bosnia, it became more proactive and focused on power-mediation and on decisive military force, increasingly refusing to adhere to multilateral rules and norms.

Overall, dramatic effects and traumatic experiences challenged both German and U.S. cultural features. This thesis also reveals that it is important to consider where to set the starting point of security culture, and that each starting point is of course an artificial construction that denies the amount of continuity of cultures over time. In the German case, the starting point can be pretty clearly set historically (1945), whereas the starting point for the examination of the U.S. security culture is blurred.

This thesis further demonstrates that the German and the U.S. security culture indeed converged in the 1990s. Specifically, the

German security culture became more similar to the U.S. security culture, mainly in regard to the use of military force. This convergence seems to contradict the trans-Atlantic rift that is widely discussed today. Yet German security culture seems regressive. Today, public and political elites show growing reticence to use force. Thus, the early lessons from World War II and the Cold War seem more formative and path-dependent than anticipated. Even though Germany contributes large military contingents to operations around the globe, German military engagement, starting with the Bosnian war, seems to resemble more the old patterns of constrained and restricted use of military force. Life in Germany seems to return to old patterns and thinking; to a foreign policy of responsibility and a culture of restraint and respective use of force. This phenomenon of German regression implies that either the Bosnian war was not a great enough contextual force to cause a permanent change of the German security culture, or, following Eckstein, the war had a sector-specific impact on German security culture, with change distributed unevenly among the different cultural components. A further great contextual force of German regression was the third Iraq war starting in March 2003. The extreme negative public opinion towards the U.S. led operation inhibited further societal support for German military engagements. It caused a resemblance to old patterns of restricted use of force.

As concerns future scholarly work on security cultures, four conclusions might be drawn. First, given that security culture is a ranked set of preferences and that the impact of exogenous factors is distributed unevenly among cultural components, the nature and structure of national security cultures are of enormous importance for further scholarly analysis. Thus, when using a comparative case study method to examine cultural change, as in this thesis, it seems wise to select most similar cases, i.e. with similar security cultures and comparable cultural preferences. In other words, the independent variable does not need to be one single historical event as long as the cultures of the cases are similar and comparable. This method might give additional insights into the nature and consistency of security cultures and how cultures change and transform irrespective of time and space. If similarities can be demonstrated, the concept of security culture consequently becomes even more important to examine and explain international foreign policy behavior.

Second, even within a ranked cultural set or menu, heterogeneity and homogeneity exist side by side. There are dominant cultural preferences and competing ones. Therefore, it is not only of importance what domestic group actually shapes the security culture of a country but also which cultural preference is more compatible with the outside world. This finding contributes to the scholarly discourse on homogeneity and heterogeneity. It implies that individuals have different orientations and learn different things from experience. Societies contain multiple strategic cultures because they encompass various subcultures. It is necessary to examine which group actually most shapes the security culture of a country, but this is in part dependent on which cultural preference is compatible with the outside world. Interdependence, globalization and integration are not yet much a part of the academic discourse on security cultures. Do nation-states share a common security culture because of parallel identity formation processes? Do liberal democracies perceive themselves as an in-group because of that? Many questions concerning transnationalism and its effects on the universality and boundaries of security cultures remain unanswered.

This thesis reveals that interdependence and multilateralism have an enormous effect on security cultures. In Germany and the U.S., the public and political elites' support for humanitarian intervention increased strongly when the UN got threatened or harassed in operations. The U.S. public especially supported use of overwhelming force after the hostage crisis and when the UN humanitarian relief operations were harassed. The German political elites and general public strongly supported the involvement of the military to safeguard the UN blue helmet mission. Even though the whole UN mission during the Bosnian war was seen as a debacle, there was a strong identification with the UN operation, and UN humanitarian aid was perceived as legitimate and morally right.

All in all, three hypotheses can be derived from the findings of this thesis:

H 1: Strong national security cultures are less vulnerable to influences from multilateral settings. On the contrary, they play a vital formative role in institutions. States with strong security cultures can strongly impact other security cultures in these multilateral settings and thus guide institutional behavior.

H 2: In using comparative case studies to examine cultural change, one may select cases with a similar security culture and thus comparable cultural preferences, rather than cases focusing on the same historical event.

H 3: It is not only important which domestic group shapes the security culture of a country, but also which cultural preferences are more compatible with the outside world in times of trial.

This thesis is not a Promethean achievement, nor does this author wish to serve a Promethean sentence. The thesis contributes to recent scholarly work, but it also raises new questions. It is evident that security cultures influence the assessment of political situations, restrain policy objectives, and condition the range of issues to which political attention is devoted. While security cultures have become a focus of recent scholarly research, proving that they are important tools for understanding foreign policy, the concept of security cultures deserves more research. The thesis enhances our understanding of German and U.S. foreign policy and sheds light on the concept of security cultures by using two case studies to compare security cultures and their persistence and change in time of war.

Friedrich Nietzsche once claimed that war is the hibernation of culture. This thesis proves that culture is neither in a torpid nor resting state in times of war. It is rather challenged and confronted with new unique experiences, which stimulate cultural change. This in turn influences and challenges political behavior during those times. Not hibernation, but acceleration of cultural change is what we observed here.

LIST OF REFERENCES

Abenheim, Donald. *Soldiers and Politics Transformed: German-American Reflections on Civil-Military Relations in a New Strategic Environment.* Berlin: Carole Hartmann Miles-Verlag, 2006.

Almond, Mark. *Europe's Backyard War: The War in the Balkans.* London: Mandarin Paperbacks, 1994.

Amnesty International. *Concerns in Europe: July-December 1995.* Amnesty International March 1996.

http://web.amnesty.org/library/pdf/EUR010011996ENGLISH/ $File/EUR0100196.pdf, 12-14; accessed 27 April 2007.

Ansel, Walter. *Hitler and the Middle Sea.* Durham, NC: Duke University Press, 1972.

Asmus, Ronald D. *Opening NATO's Door: How the Alliance Remade Itself for a New Era.* New York: Columbia University Press, 2002.

Bailey, Ronald H. *Partisans and Guerillas.* Alexandria, VA: Time-Life Books, 1978.

Barzini, Luigi. *The Europeans.* New York: Simon and Schuster, 1983.

Beelman, Maud S. "Hear No Evil, See No Evil: Early U.S. Policy in Yugoslavia." *APF Reporter* 18, no. 1.

http://www.aliciapatterson.org/APF1801/Beelman/Beelman.html, accessed 27 April 2007.

Belknap, Margaret H. *The CNN Effect: Strategic Enabler or Operational Risk?* U.S. Army War College, Strategy Research Project, 2001.

Bennet, Christopher. *Yugoslavia's Bloody Collapse: Causes, Course and Consequences.* New York: New York University Press, 1995.

Biagi, Shirley. *An Introduction to Mass Media.* Toronto: Thomson Wadsworth, 2005.

Biermann, Rafael. "Back to the Roots: The European Community and the Dissolution of Yugoslavia – Policies under the Impact of Global Sea-Change." In *Journal of European Integration History* 10, no. 1, 29-51. Baden-Baden: Nomos Verlagsgesellschaft, 2004.

Biermann, Rafael: *Lehrjahre im Kosovo: Das Scheitern der internationalen Krisenprävention vor Kriegsausbruch.* Paderborn: Ferdinand Schöningh, 2006.

Booth, Ken. *Strategy and Ethnocentrism.* New York: Holmes and Meyer Publishers, 1979.

Brands, W. H. *What America Owes the World.* Cambridge: Cambridge University Press, 2000.

Brodie, Bernard. *Strategy in the Missile Age.* Princeton: Princeton University Press, 1959.

Brown, Michael E. "The Causes of Internal Conflict: An Overview." In *Nationalism and Ethnic Conflict*, edited by Michael E. Brown et al., 3-26. Cambridge, MA: MIT Press, 2001.

Bundesministerium der Verteidigung. *Weißbuch 1994: Weißbuch zur Sicherheit der Bundesrepublik Deutschland und zur Lage und Zukunft der Bundeswehr.* Bundesministerium der Verteidigung im Auftrag der Bundesregierung, 1994.

Burger, Rudolf. "Nationale Ethik: Illusion und Realitaet," *Hamburger Ausblicke* 2 (2006),

http://archiv.hausrissen.org/pdf/ausblicke/2-2006/Burger%20-%20Nationale%20Interessen.pdf; accessed 27 April 2007.

Bush, George H. W. *Address at the West Point Military Academy*, United States Military Academy, West Point, NY, January 5, 1993.

Cate, Fred H. "'CNN effect' is Not Clear-Cut," *Humanitarian Affairs Review* (Summer 2002),

http://www.globalpolicy.org/ngos/aid/2002/summercnn.htm; accessed 27 April 2007.

Center on Military History. *German Antiguerilla Operations in the Balkans (1941-1944).* Washington D.C.: U.S. Government Printing Office, 1989.

Collmer, Sabine. "'All politics is local': Deutsche Sicherheits- und Verteidigungspolitik im Spiegel der Oeffentlichen Meinung," In *Deutsche Sicherheitspolitik: Eine Bilanz der Regierung Schroeder,* edited by Sebastian Harnisch, Christos Katsioulis, and Marco Overhaus, 201-25. Baden-Baden: Nomos Verlagsgesellschaft, 2004.

Commission of the European Communities. *Eurobarometer: Public Opinion in the European Community, Nr. 37.* Brussels: Directorate-General Information, Communication, Culture. Surveys, Research, Analyses (June 1992).

Commission of the European Communities. *Eurobarometer: Public Opninion in the European Community, Nr. 38.* Brussels: Directorate-General Information, Communication, Culture. Surveys, Research, Analyses (December 1992).

Commission of the European Communities. *Eurobarometer: Public Opninion in the European Community, Nr. 40.* Brussels: Directorate-General Information, Communication, Culture. Surveys, Research, Analyses (December 1993).

Craig, Gordon A. *The Politics of the Prussian Army 1640-1945.* New York: Oxford University Press, 1955.

Craig, Gordon A., and Alexander L. George. *Force and Statecraft: Diplomatic Problems of Our Time, 3rd ed.* New York: Oxford University Press, 1995.

Cviic, Christopher. *Remaking the Balkans.* New York: Council on Foreign Relations Press, 1991.

Daalder, Ivo H. *Getting to Dayton: The Making of America's Bosnia Policy.* Washington, D.C.: Brookings Institution Press, 2000.

Daalder, Ivo H. "Prospects for Global Leadership Sharing: The Security Dimension." In *Maryland/Tsukuba Papers on U.S.-Japan Relations* edited by I. M. Destler and Hideo Sato, Center for International and Security Studies at Maryland (CISSM) School of Public Affairs (July 1996).

Doeneke, Justus D. *Storm on the Horizon: The Challenge to American Intervention, 1939-1941.* Lanham: Rowman and Littlefield Publishers, 2003.

Dorff, Robert H. "German Policy Toward Peace Support Operations." In *Force, Statecraft and German Unity: The Struggle to Adapt Institutions and Practices.* Strategic Studies Institute, US Army War College, Carlisle Barracks, PA (December 1996).

Dowty, Alan, and Gil Loescher. "Refugee Flows as Grounds for International Action." In *Nationalism and Ethnic Conflict: Revised Edition*, edited by Michael E. Brown et al., 337-66. Cambridge, MA: MIT Press, 2001.

Drakulic, Slavenka. "Women Hide Behind a Wall of Silence." In *Why Bosnia? Writings on the Balkan War*, edited by Rabia Ali and Lawrence Lifschultz, 112-131. Stony Creek, Connecticut: Pamphleteer's Press, 1993.

Dueck, Colin. *Reluctant Crusaders: Power, Culture, and Change in American Grand Strategy*. Princeton: Princeton University Press, 2006.

Duffield, John S. *World Power Forsaken: Political Culture, International Institutions and German Security Policy After Unification*. Stanford: Stanford University Press, 1998.

Eckstein, Harry. "A Culturalist Theory of Political Change." *American Political Science Review* 82, no. 3 (Sept. 1998): 789-804.

Eyal, Jonathan. *Europe and Yugoslavia: Lessons from a Failure*. London: Royal United Services for Defence Studies, 1993.

Farkas, Evelyn N. *Fractured States and U.S. Foreign Policy: Iraq, Ethiopia, and Bosnia in the 1990s*. New York: Palgrave MacMillan, 2003.

Farrel, Theo. "Constructivist Security Studies: Portrait of a Research Program." *International Studies Review* 4, no. 1 (2002): 49-72.

Farrel, Theo. "Strategic Culture and American Empire." *SAIS Review* 25.2 (2005): 3-18.

Finnemore, Martha. "Constructing Norms of Humanitarian Intervention." In *The Culture of National Security Norms and Identity in World Politics*, edited by Peter J. Katzenstein, 153-185. New York: Columbia University Press, 1996.

Gagnon, V.P. Jr. "Ethnic Nationalism and International Conflict: The Case of Serbia." *International Security* 19, no. 3 (Winter 1994): 130-166.

Gates, Robert M. *From the Shadows: The Ultimate Insider's Account of Five Presidents and How They Won the Cold War*. New York: Simon and Schuster, 1996.

Glenny, Misha. *The Balkan: Nationalism, War, and the Great Powers, 1804-1999*. New York: Viking, 2000.

Goedde, Petra. *GIs and Germans: Culture, Gender and Foreign Relations, 1945-1949*. New Haven: Yale University Press, 2003.

Goertz, Gary, and Paul F. Diehl. "The Initiation and Termination of Enduring Rivalries: The Impact of Political Shocks." *American Journal of Political Science* 39, no. 1 (1995) 30-52.

Gow, James. *Triumph of the Lack of Will: International Diplomacy and the Yugoslav War*. New York: Columbia University Press, 1997.

Gray, Chris Hables. *Postmodern War: The New Politics of Conflict*. London: Routledge, 1997.

Gray, Colin S. *Modern Strategy*. Oxford: Oxford University Press, 1999.

Gray, Colin S. "Strategy in the Nuclear Age: The United States, 1945-1991." In *The Making of Strategy: Rulers, States, and War*, edited by Williamson Murray, MacGregor Knox, and Alvin H. Bernstein, 579-613. New York: Cambridge University Press, 1994.

Grundsatzprogramm der Sozialdemokratischen Partei Deutschlands. http://www.spdschleswigholstein.de/docs/1118733935_program mdebatte_grundsatzprogramm.pdf; accessed 27 April 2007.

Guttmann, Allen, ed. *Korea: Cold War and Limited War*, 2nd ed. New York: D. C. Heath, 1972.

Hanrieder, Wolfram. "Compatibility and Consensus: A Proposal for the Conceptual Linkage of External and Internal Dimensions of Foreign Policy." *American Political Science Review* 61, no. 4 (Dec. 1967).

Haftendorn, Helga. *Deutsche Aussenpolitik zwischen Selbstbeschränkung und Selbstbehauptung 1945-2000*. Muenchen: Deutsche Verlagsanstalt, 2001.

Haftendorn, Helga. "Gulliver in der Mitte Europas: Internationale Verflechtung und nationale Handlungsmöglichkeiten." In *Deutschlands neue Außenpolitik. Band 1: Grundlagen*, edited by Karl Kaiser, Hans W. Maull, and Gabriele Brenke. München: Oldenbourg, 1994.

Harper, John Lamberton. *American Visions of Europe*. Cambridge: Cambridge University Press, 1996.

Hilz, Wolfram. *Europas verhindertes Führungstrio: Die Sicherheitspolitik Deutschlands, Frankreichs und Großbritanniens in den Neunzigern.* Paderborn: Ferdinand Schöningh, 2005.

Hinckley, Ronald H. *People, Polls, and Policymakers: American Public Opinion and National Security.* New York: Lexington Books, 1992.

Hobsbawm, Eric. *The Age of Extremes: A History of the World, 1914-1991.* New York: Vintage Books, 1996.

Hogan, Michael J. *A Cross of Iron: Harry S. Truman and the Origins of the National Security State 1945-1954.* New York: Cambridge University Press, 1998.

Holbrooke, Richard C. *To End a War.* New York: Random House, 1998.

Howlett, Darryl. "Strategic Culture: Reviewing Recent Literature." *Strategic Insights* 4, no. 10 (2005), http://www.ccc.nps.navy.mil/si/2005/Oct/howlettOct05.asp; accessed 27 April 2007.

Huntington, Samuel P. *The Soldier and the State: The Theory and Practice of Civil-Military Relations.* Cambridge, MA: Belknap Press, 1957.

Hurst, Steven. *The Foreign Policy of the Bush Administration: In Search of a New World Order.* New York: Cassel, 1999.

Jacobsen, Hans Adolf. *Drei Jahrzehnte Assenpolitik der DDR: Bestimmungsfaktoren, Instrumente, Aktionsfelder.* München: Oldenbourg Verlag, 1979.

Johnston, Alistair Iain. "Thinking about Strategic Culture." *International Security* 19, no. 4 (Spring 1995): 32-64.

Johnston, Karin. "German Public Opinion and the Crisis in Bosnia." In *International Public Opinion and the Bosnia Crisis,* edited by Richard Sobel and Eric Shiraev, 249-281. New York: Lexington Books, 2003.

Jomini. *The Art of War.* Westport: Greenwood Press.

Jordan, Robert S. *Norstad: Cold War NATO Supreme Commander: Airman, Strategist, Diplomat.* New York: St. Martin's Press, Inc., 2000.

Kagan, Robert. *Of Paradise and Power: America and Europe in the New World Order.* New York: Vintage, 2003.

140

Kaiser, Karl, and Hans W. Maull, eds. *Deutschlands neue Außenpolitik: Band 1: Grundlagen.* München: Oldenbourg, 1994.

Kaplan, Robert D. *Balkan Ghosts: A Journey through History.* New York: St. Martin's Press, 1993.

Kaser, Karl. "Das ethnische ,engineering'." In *Der Jugoslawien-Krieg Handbuch zu Vorgeschichte: Verlauf und Konsequenzen,* edited by Dunja Melcic, 408-22. Wiesbaden: Westdeutscher Verlag, 1999.

Kennan, George F. *American Diplomacy,* expanded edition. Chicago: University of Chicago Press, 1984.

Kielinger, Thomas, and Max Otte. "Germany--The Pressured Power." *Foreign Policy* 91, no. 2 (1993): 44-62.

Kommission der Europaeischen Gemeinschaft. *Eurobarometer: Die oeffentliche Meinung der Europaeischen Gemeinschaft, Nr. 35.* Bruessel: Generaldirektion Information, Kommunikation, Kultur. Umfragen, Forschung, Analysen (June 1991).

Kommission der Europaeischen Gemeinschaft. *Eurobarometer: Die oeffentliche Meinung der Europaeischen Gemeinschaft, Nr. 36.* Bruessel: Generaldirektion Information, Kommunikation, Kultur. Umfragen, Forschung, Analysen (December 1991).

Krasner, Stephen. "Approaches to the State: Alternative Conceptions and Alternative Dynamics." *Comparative Politics* 16, no. 2 (1984), 223-46.

Krell, Gert. "Wie der Gewalt widerstehen? Konflik-intervention und die Frage legitimer Gegengewalt als ethisches und politisches Problem." In *Der Krieg in Bosnien und das hilflose Europa / Plädoyer für eine militärische UN-Intervention,* 12-22. Frankfurt aM: Hessische Friedens- und Konfliktforschung, 1993.

Kull, Steven, and Clay Ramsay. *U.S. Public Attitudes on U.S. Involvement in Bosnia,* Program on International Policy Attitudes, CISSM, School of Public Affairs, University of Maryland, May 4, 1994.

Kull, Steven, and Clay Ramsay. "U.S. Public Opinion on Intervention in Bosnia." In *International Public Opinion and the Bosnia Crisis,* edited by Richard Sobel and Eric Shiraev, 69-106. New York: Lexington Books, 2003.

Kull, Steven, and Clay Ramsay. *U.S. Public Opinion on Intervention in Bosnia.* Program on International Policy Attitudes, CISSM, School of Public Affairs, University of Maryland, May 15, 1993.

Lantis, Jeffrey S. "Strategic Culture from Clausewitz to Constructivism." *Strategic Insights* 4, no. 10 (2005), http://www.ccc.nps.navy.mil/si/2005/Oct/lantisOct05.asp.

Lantis, Jeffrey S. *Strategic Dilemmas and the Evolution of German Foreign Policy since Unification.* Westport: Praeger Publishers, 2002.

Lantis, Jeffrey S. "The Moral Imperative of Force: The Evolution of German Strategic Culture in Kosovo." *Comparative Strategy,* no. 21 (2002): 21-46.

Larres, Klaus. "Bloody as Hell." In *Journal of European Integration History* 10, no. 1, 179-202. Baden-Baden: Nomos Verlagsgesellschaft, 2004.

Levy, Jack S. "Learning and Foreign Policy: Sweeping a Conceptual Minefield." *International Organization* 48, no. 2 (Spring 1994): 279-312.

Libal, Michael. "The Road to Recognition: Germany, the EC and the Disintegration of Yugoslavia 1991." In *Journal of European Integration History* 10, no. 1, 75-96. Baden-Baden: Nomos Verlagsgesellschaft, 2004.

Lind, Michael. *The American Way of Strategy.* New York: Oxford University Press, 2006.

Link, Arthur S. *Woodrow Wilson: Revolution, War, and Peace.* Arlington Heights, IL: AHM Publisher Corp., 1979.

Linn, Brian M. *"The American Way of War* Revisited." *Journal of Military History* 66, no. 2 (April 2002): 501-533.

Lippmann, Walter. *Public Opinion and Foreign Policy in the United States.* London: Allen and Unwin, 1952.

Livingston, Steve. "'The CNN Effect': How 24-Hour News Coverage Affects Government Decisions and Public Opinion." In *A Brookings/Harvard Forum: Press Coverage and the War on Terrorism,* January 2002.

Maull, Hanns. "Zivilmacht Bundesrepublik: Vierzehn Thesen für eine neue deutsche Aussenpolitik." *Europa-Archiv* 47, no. 1 (1992): 269-278.

Mearsheimer, John J. "Back to the Future: Instability in Europe after the Cold War." *International Security* 15, no. 1 (Summer 1990): 5-56.

Meier, Viktor. "Die politische Bedeutung der Medien in der Konfliktbewaeltigung." In *Deutsche Konfliktbewaeltigung auf dem Balkan. Erfahrungen und Lehren aus dem Einsatz,* edited by Rafael Biermann, 139-150. Baden-Baden: Nomos Verlagsgesellschaft, 2002.

Melcic, Dunja. *Der Jugoslawienkrieg Handbuch zur Vorgeschichte und Konsequenzen.* Wiesbaden: Westdeutscher Verlag, 1999.

Mennel, Rainer. *Der Balkan: Einfluss und Interessensphœren.* Osnabrueck: Biblio Verlag, 1999.

Menon, Anand. *France, NATO and the Limits of Independence 1981-1997: The Politics of Ambivalence.* New York: St. Martin's Press, Inc., 2000.

Mermin, Jonathan. *Debating War and Peace: Media Coverage of U.S. Intervention in the Post-Vietnam Era.* Princeton: Princeton University Press, 1999.

Millett, Allan R. et al. *For the Common Defense: A Military History of the United States of America.* New York: Free Press, 1984.

Millis,Walter ed. *American Military Thought.* New York: Bobbs-Merrill, 1966.

Mills, Nicolaus. *The new Killing Fields: Massacre and the Politics of Intervention.* New York: Basic Books, 2002.

Minear, Larry, Colin Scott, and Thomas George Weiss. *The News Media, Civil War, and Humanitarian Action.* Boulder: Lynne Riener Publishers, 1996.

Mockaitis, Thomas R. *Peace Operations and Intrastate Conflict: The Sword or the Olive Branch.* Westport: Praeger Publishers, 1999.

Morgenthau, Hans J. *Politics among Nations.* Chicago: University of Chicago Press, 1948.

Moskos, Charles. "Grave Decision: When Americans Accept Casualties." *Chicago Tribune.* December 12, 1998.

Noelle-Neumann, Elisabeth, and Renate Köcher, eds. *Allensbacher Jahrbuch der Demoskopie*. München: K. G. Saur, 1993.

Noelle-Neumann, Elisabeth, and Renate Köcher, eds. *Allensbacher Jahrbuch der Demoskopie*. München: K.G.Saur, 1997.

Nolte, Georg. "Germany: Ensuring Political Legitimacy for the Use of Military Forces by Requiring Constitutional Accountability." In *Democratic Accountability and the Use of Force in International Law*, edited by Charlotte Ku and Harold K. Jacobsen, 231-253. New York: Cambridge University Press, 2002.

Nuechterlein, Donald E. *America Recommitted: A Superpower Assesses Its Role in a Turbulent World,* 2nd Edition. Lexington: University Press of Kentucky, 2001.

Nye, Joseph S., Jr. "U.S. Power and Strategy after Iraq." *Foreign Affairs* 82, no. 4 (2003): 60-73.

Otte, Max. *A Rising Middle Power? German Foreign Policy in Transformation, 1989-1999*. New York: St. Martin's Press, 2000.

Paret, Peter et al. eds. *Makers of Modern Strategy: From Machiavelli to the Nuclear Age*. Princeton: Princeton University Press, 1986.

Paulsen, Thomas. *Die Jugoslawienpolitik der USA 1989-1994*. Baden-Baden: Nomos Verlagsgesellschaft, 1995.

Payne, Richard J. *The Clash with Distant Cultures: Values, Interests, and Force in American Foreign Policy*. Albany: State University of New York Press, 1995.

Pfaff, William. "Invitation to War." *Foreign Affairs* 72, no. 3 (Summer 1993): 97-109.

Philippi, Nina. *Bundeswehr-Auslandseinsaetze als aussen- und sicherheitspolitisches Problem des geeinten Deutschland*. Frankfurt a.M.: Peter Lang Publishing Inc., 1997.

Rathfelder, Erich. "Der Krieg an seinen Schauplätzen." In *Der Jugoslawien-Krieg Handbuch zu Vorgeschichte, Verlauf und Konsequenzen*, edited by Dunja Melcic, 345-63. Wiesbaden: Westdeutscher Verlag, 1999.

Risse-Kappen, Thomas. *Cooperation among Democracies: The European Influence on U.S. Foreign Policy*. Princeton, Princeton University Press, 1995.

Rosati, Jerel A. "A Cognitive Approach to the Study of Foreign Policy." In *Foreign Policy Analysis, Continuity and Change in Its Second Generation*, edited by Laura Neack, Jeanne A. K. Hey, and Patrick J. Haney, 52- 63. Englewood Cliffs: Prentice Hall, 1995.

Russet, Bruce M., et al. *Grasping the Democratic Peace Principles for a Post Cold War World*. Princeton: Princeton University Press, 1993.

Sapolsky, Harvey M., and Jeremy Shapiro. "Casualties, Technology, and America's Future Wars." *Parameters* (Sept. 1996): 119-127.

Schild, Georg. "Amerikas Aussenpolitischer Pragmatismus." *Aussenpolitik* 46, no. 1 (Quartal 1, 1995): 31-39.

Schmuck-Soldan, Steffen."Der Pazifismus bei Buendnis 90/ Die Gruenen: Entwicklung und Stellenwert einer aussenpolitischen Ideologie 1990-2000." PhD diss., Philosophische Fakultät III der Humboldt-Universität zu Berlin, 2004.

Schoch, Bruno. "Anerkennen als Ersatzhandlung / Ein kritischer Rückblick auf die Bonner Jugoslawienpolitik." In *Der Krieg in Bosnien das hilflose Europa / Plädoyer für eine militärissche UN-Intervention*, edited by Hessische Stiftung Friedens- und Konfliktforschung. Frankfurt aM (1993).

Scholtyseck, Joachim. *Die Außenpolitik der DDR*. München: Oldenbourg Wissenschaftsverlag, 2003.

Schwegmann, Christoph. "The Contact Group and its Impact on the European Institutional Structure." *Occasional Papers 16*. The Institute for Security Studies Western European Union (June 2000).

Seidt, Hans-Ulrich. "Führung in der Krise? Die Balkankriege und das deutsche Konfliktmanagement." In *Deutsche Konfliktbewältigung auf dem Balkan: Erfahrungen und Lehren aus dem Einsatz*, edited by Rafael Biermann, 39-56. Baden-Baden: Nomos Verlagsgesellschaft, 2002.

Sells, Michael A. *The Bridge Betrayed: Religion and Genocide in Bosnia*. Berkeley: University of California Press, 1996.

Siedschlag, Alexander. *Die aktive Beteiligung Deutschlands an miliaerischen Aktionen zur Verwirklichung Kollektiver Sicherheit*. Frankfurt a.M.: Peter Lang Publishing Inc., 1995.

Silber, Laura, and Alan Little. *Yugoslavia: Death of a Nation*. New York: TV Books, 1996.

Simes, Dimitri K. "America's Imperial Dilemma." *Foreign Affairs* 82, no. 6 (2003): 91-102.

Snyder, Jack. *The Soviet Strategic Culture: Implications for Nuclear Options.* Report number R-2154-AF. Santa Monica, Calif.: Rand Cooperation, 1977.

Sobel, Richard, and Eric Shiraev, eds. *International Public Opinion and the Bosnia Crisis.* New York: Lexington Books, 2003.

Sontheimer, Kurt, and Wilhelm Bleek. *Die DDR: Politik Gesellschaft, Wirtschaft.* Hamburg: Hoffmann und Kampe, 1979.

Stone, Elizabeth L., Christopher P. Twomey, and Peter R. Lavoy. "Comparative Strategic Culture." *Strategic Insights* 4, no. 10 (2005), http://www.ccc.nps.navy.mil/events/recent/ComparativeStrategi cCultureSep05rpt.asp; accessed 27 April 2007.

Summers, Harry G., Jr. *On Strategy: A Critical Analysis of the Vietnam War.* New York: Dell Books, 1982.

Szabo, Stephen F. *Parting Ways: The Crisis in German-American Relations.* Washington D.C.: Brookings Institution Press, 2004.

Tannenwald, Nina. "Stigmatizing the Bomb: Origins of the Nuclear Taboo." *International Security* 29, no. 4 (Spring 2005): 5-49.

Thomas, Dorothy Q., and E. Ralph Regan. "Rape in War: Challenging the Tradition of Impunity." *SAIS Review* (1994): 82-99.

Thomas, Ian Q. R. *The Promise of the Alliance: NATO and the Political Imagination.* Lanham: Rowman and Littlefield, 1997.

Tomasevich, Jozo. *War and Revolution in Yugoslavia: Occupation and Collaboration, 1941-1945.* Stanford: Stanford University Press, 2001.

Upton, Emory. *The Military Policy of the United States.* New York: Greenwood, 1968.

Van Evera, Stephen. "Hypothesis on Nationalism and War." In *Nationalism and Ethnic Conflict*, edited by Michael E. Brown et al., 26-61.Cambridge, MA: MIT Press, 2001.

Vitas, Robert A., and John Allen Williams, eds. *U.S. National Security Policy and Strategy 1987-1994: Documents and Policy Proposals.* Westport: Greenwood Press, 1996.

Walker, Jenonne. "Keeping America in Europe." *Foreign Policy*, 83 (Summer 1991): 128-142.

Walker, Thomas. "American Uniqueness, Strategic Culture and the Origins of the Transatlantic Rift." Paper presented at the International Studies Association meetings, Chicago, March, 2007.

Wallander, Celeste A., and Robert O. Keohane. "Risk, Threat, and Security Institutions." In *Imperfect Union: Security Institutions over Time and Space*, edited by Helga Haftendorn, Robert O. Keohane and Celeste A. Wallander, 21-47. New York: Oxford University Press, 1999.

Weigley, Russell F. *The American Way of War: A History of United States Military Strategy and Policy*. Bloomington: Indiana University Press, 1973.

Woodward, C. Vann. "The Age of Reinterpretation." *American Historical Review* 66, no. 1 (Oct. 1960): 1-19.

Woodward, Susan. *Balkan Tragedy: Chaos and Dissolution after the Cold War*. Washington D.C.: Brookings Institution, 1995.

Zapantis, Andrew L. *Hitler's Balkan Campaign and the Invasion of the USSR*. New York: Columbia University Press, 1987.

ACKNOWLEDGMENTS

I would like to thank Professor Rafael Biermann and Professor Donald Abenheim for their ongoing support and guidance as thesis advisors and for sharing their tremendous amount of knowledge in various seminars throughout the past twelve months. I further would like to thank Professor Debra Rosenthal for the excellent work editing my thesis and finally I thank CDR Travis Owens for his good friendship and his support to me and my family, in order to make our stay in the United States of America as pleasant as possible.

Special thanks go to my wife, Karin for her enduring patience and understanding, providing the basis for the success in my study and thesis alike, and my son Paul for his enduring impatience which forced me to focus on other things than study and this thesis.

Carola Hartmann Miles-Verlag

Militär und Gesellschaft

Hans-Christian Beck, Christian Singer (Hrsg.), *Entscheiden – Führen – Verantworten. Soldatsein im 21. Jahrhundert,* Berlin 2011.

Wolf Graf von Baudissin, *Grundwert Frieden in Politik – Strategie – Führung von Streitkräften,* hrsg. von Claus von Rosen, Berlin 2014.

Marcel Bohnert, Lukas J. Reitstetter (Hrsg.), *Armee im Aufbruch. Zur Gedankenwelt junger Offiziere in den Kampftruppen der Bundeswehr,* Berlin 2014.

Phil C. Langer, Gerhard Kümmel (Hrsg.), *„Wir sind Bundeswehr." Wie viel Vielfalt benötigen/vertragen die Streitkräfte?,* Berlin 2015.

Eberhard Birk, Peter Andreas Popp (Hrsg.), *Luftwaffenoffizier 21. Das Selbstverständnis des Luftwaffenoffiziers zu Beginn des 21. Jahrhunderts, (aus der Reihe Schriften zur Geschichte der Deutschen Luftwaffe, Band 5),* Berlin 2016.

Alois Bach, Walter Sauer (Hrsg.), *Schützen. Retten. Kämpfen. Dienen für Deutschland,* Berlin 2016.

Marcel Bohnert, Björn Schreiber (Hrsg.), *Die unsichtbaren Veteranen. Kriegsheimkehrer in der deutschen Gesellschaft,* Berlin 2016.

Angelika Dörfler-Dierken (Hrsg.), *Hinschauen! Geschlecht, Rechtspopulismus, Rituale: Systemische Probleme oder individuelles Fehlverhalten?,* Berlin 2019.

Schriften zur Tradition

Eberhard Birk, Winfried Heinemann, Sven Lange (Hrsg.), *Tradition für die Bundeswehr. Neue Aspekte einer alten Debatte,* Berlin 2012.

Donald Abenheim, Uwe Hartmann (Hrsg.), *Tradition in der Bundeswehr. Zum Erbe des deutschen Soldaten und zur Umsetzung des neuen Traditionserlasses,* Berlin 2018.

Joachim Welz, *Vom Kontingentsheer zum Reichsheer: Militärkonventionen als Motor der Wehrverfassung,* Berlin 2018.

Donald Abenheim, Uwe Hartmann, *Einführung in die Tradition der Bundeswehr. Das soldatische Erbe in dem besten Deutschland, das es je gab,* Berlin 2019.

Eberhard Birk, Heiner Möllers (Hrsg.), *Die Luftwaffe und ihre Traditionen (aus der Reihe Schriften zur Geschichte der Deutschen Luftwaffe, Band 10),* Berlin 2019.

Hans-Günter Behrendt (Hrsg.): *Erinnerungsorte der Bundeswehr – Personen, Ereignisse und Institutionen der soldatischen Traditionspflege,* Berlin 2020.

Erinnerungen

Heinz Laube, *Duell am Himmel,* Berlin 2016.

Viktor Toyka, *Dienst in Zeiten des Wandels. Erinnerungen aus 40 Jahren Dienst als Marineoffizier 1966-2000,* Berlin 2017.

Hans-Eckhard Tribess (Hrsg.), *Im Leben unterwegs – für den Frieden. Festschrift für Wolfgang Altenburg zum 90. Geburtstag am 22. Juni 2018,* Berlin 2019.

Kurt Graf v. Schweinitz, *Notizen im Transit von Krieg und Frieden,* Berlin 2020.

Militärgeschichte

Eberhard Kliem, Kathrin Orth, *"Wir wurden wie blödsinnig vom Feind beschossen". Menschen und Schiffe in der Skagerrakschlacht 1916,* Berlin 2016.

Hans Frank, Norbert Rath, *Kommodore Rudolf Petersen. Führer der Schnellboote 1942–1945. Ein Leben in Licht und Schatten unteilbarer Verantwortung,* Berlin 2016.

Ingo Pfeiffer, *Heinz Neukirchen. Marinekarriere an wechselnden Fronten,* Berlin 2017.

Joachim Welz, *Erfolgsstory oder Trauma – die Übernahme von Armeen. Lehren aus der Übernahme des österreichischen Bundesheeres in die Wehrmacht 1938 und der Reste der NVA in die Bundeswehr 1990,* Berlin 2018.

Georg Neuhaus, *Am Anfang war ein Speer. Eine Chronographie der Kriegs- und Militärtechnologien,* Berlin 2018.

Hans-Werner Ahrens, *Die Transportflieger der Luftwaffe 1956 bis 197. Konzeption – Aufbau – Einsatz, (Reihe Schriften zur Geschichte der Deutschen Luftwaffe, Band 8)*, Berlin 2019.

Jobst Reller, *Die Anfänge der evangelischen Militärseelsorge*, Berlin 2019.

Eberhard Frhr. v. Senden, Friedrich Frhr. v. Senden, *Der Erste Weltkrieg 1914–1918. Erlebnisse eines jungen Leutnants*, Berlin 2020.

Jahrbuch Innere Führung (seit 2009)

Uwe Hartmann, Claus von Rosen (Hrsg.), *Jahrbuch Innere Führung 2018. Innere Führung zwischen Aufbruch, Abbau und Abschaffung: Neues denken, Mitgestaltung fördern, Alternativen wagen*, Berlin 2018.

Uwe Hartmann, Claus von Rosen (Hrsg.), *Jahrbuch Innere Führung 2019. Bundeswehr im Aufbruch. Hindernisse von den verteidigungspolitischen Vorstellungen der AFD bis zu den sicherheitspolitischen Meinungen in der Zivilgesellschaft*, Berlin 2019.

Standpunkte und Orientierungen

Hartwig von Schubert, *Integrative Militärethik. Ethische Urteilsbildung in der militärischen Führung*, Berlin 2015.

Uwe Hartmann, *Hybrider Krieg als neue Bedrohung von Freiheit und Frieden. Zur Relevanz der Inneren Führung in Politik, Gesellschaft und Streitkräften*, Berlin 2015.

Klaus Beckmann, *Treue.Bürgermut.Ungehorsam. Anstöße zur Führungskultur und zum beruflichen Selbstverständnis in der Bundeswehr*, Berlin 2015.

Uwe Hartmann, *Der gute Soldat. Politische Kultur und soldatisches Selbstverständnis heute*, Berlin 2018.

Christian Bauer, Marcel Bohnert, Jan Pahl, *Vitalis Innere Führung! Zum Status Quo der Führungskultur in den deutschen Streitkräften*, Berlin 2018.

Helmut Jermer, *Innere Führung kompakt. Eine Zusammenschau als Lehr- und Lernhilfe*, Berlin 2019.

Monterey Studies

Uwe Hartmann, *Carl von Clausewitz and the Making of Modern Strategy*, Potsdam 2002.

Frank Reimers, *Security Culture in Times of War: How did the Balkan War affect the Security Cultures in Germany and the United States?*, Berlin 2007 (²2020).

Frank Hagemann, *Strategy Making in the European Union*, Berlin 2010.

Ralf Hammerstein, *Deliberalization in Jordan: the Roles of Islamists and U.S.-EU Assistance in stalled Democratization*, Berlin 2011.

Jochen Wittmann, *Auftragstaktik*, Berlin 2012.

Michael Hanisch, *On German Foreign und Security Policy. Determinants of German Military Engagement in Africa since 2011*, Berlin 2015.

Grégoire Monnet, *The Evolution of Strategic Thought Since September 11, 2001*, Berlin 2016.

Stefan Klein, *America First? Isolationism in U.S. Foreign Policy from the 19th to the 21st Century*, Berlin 2017.

Torsten Gojowsky, Sebastian Kögler, *Building Special Operations Relationships with Fragile Partners. Best practices from Iraq, Syria, and Afghanistan*, Berlin 2019.

Darell Moyers, *Frontline Leadership – Leadership Advice for USAF Junior Officers, Mid-Grade Officers & NCOs*, Berlin 2020.

Offiziersbibliothek

Uwe Hartmann, *Offiziersbibliothek I: Deutschland*, Berlin 2020.

www.miles-verlag.jimdo.com